W9-BOB-394

# Welcome

**The sparkle**, warmth and joy of the holiday season make it unlike any other time of year. *Country Woman Christmas 2010* captures that Yuletide magic—and it's all here for you!

The latest edition in a cherished annual series, this merry treasury gives you festive foods, decorations and gifts to make the season as bright as can be. Savor 103 scrumptious recipes for your holiday feast, cookie tray and more...dazzling do-it-yourself accents for your home...handcrafted gifts you can easily make...even a charming Nutcracker Ballet Party for kids.

Plus, you'll enjoy a divine gingerbread church, heartwarming Christmas stories and much, much more. Happy holidays!

20

110

48

# Country Woman
# *Christmas*
## 2010

## ON THE COVER
Gingerbread Country Church, p. 74

## Share Your Holiday Joy

DO YOU celebrate Christmas in a special way? If so, we'd like to know! We're already gathering material for the next edition of *Country Woman Christmas*. And we need your help!

Does your family carry on a Yuletide tradition? Or do you deck your halls in some festive way? Maybe you know of a Christmas-loving country woman others might like to meet.

Do you have a nostalgic or inspirational story to share? Perhaps you've written holiday poetry or fiction. We'd also like *original* Christmas quilt patterns and craft projects, plus handmade gifts, decorations, etc. And don't forget to include your best-loved recipes for holiday main courses, side dishes, appetizers, desserts, breads, cookies, candies, etc.

Send your ideas and photos to "CW Christmas Book," 5400 S. 60th Street, Greendale WI 53129. (Enclose a self-addressed stamped envelope if you'd like materials returned.) Or E-mail your ideas and photos to *bookeditors@reimanpub.com* (write "CW Christmas" on the subject line).

©2010 Reiman Media Group, Inc.
5400 S. 60th St., Greendale WI 53129
All rights reserved.

Taste of Home is a registered trademark of The Reader's Digest Association, Inc.

SENIOR VICE PRESIDENT, EDITOR IN CHIEF: Catherine Cassidy

VICE PRESIDENT, EXECUTIVE EDITOR/BOOKS: Heidi Reuter Lloyd

FOOD DIRECTOR: Diane Werner RD

SENIOR EDITOR/BOOKS: Mark Hagen

EDITOR: Michelle Bretl

ASSOCIATE EDITOR: Amy Glander

CRAFT EDITOR: Jane Craig

FOOD EDITOR: Wendy Stenman

ART DIRECTOR: Rudy Krochalk

CONTENT PRODUCTION SUPERVISOR: Julie Wagner

DESIGN LAYOUT ARTIST: Nancy Novak

PROOFREADER: Linne Bruskewitz

RECIPE ASSET SYSTEM MANAGER: Coleen Martin

PREMEDIA SUPERVISOR: Scott Berger

RECIPE TESTING AND EDITING: Taste of Home Test Kitchen

FOOD PHOTOGRAPHY: Reiman Photo Studio

ADMINISTRATIVE ASSISTANT: Barb Czysz

COVER PHOTO PHOTOGRAPHER: Rob Hagen

COVER FOOD STYLIST: Sarah Thompson

COVER SET STYLIST: Deone Jahnke

NORTH AMERICAN CHIEF MARKETING OFFICER: Lisa Karpinski

VICE PRESIDENT/BOOK MARKETING: Dan Fink

CREATIVE DIRECTOR/CREATIVE MARKETING: Jim Palmen

**The Reader's Digest Association, Inc.**
PRESIDENT AND CHIEF EXECUTIVE OFFICER: Mary G. Berner

PRESIDENT, NORTH AMERICAN AFFINITIES: Suzanne M. Grimes

International Standard Book Number (10): 0-89821-799-7

International Standard Book Number (13): 978-0-89821-799-5

International Standard Serial Number: 1093-6750

*Timeless Recipes from Trusted Home Cooks®* is a registered trademark of Reiman Media Group, Inc.

Printed in U.S.A.

For other Taste of Home books and products, visit ShopTasteofHome.com.

# Christmas
## DECORATING

*Make merry all season long with the creative, quick, do-it-yourself ideas in this chapter.*

# A Tree with Personality

*Decorate a miniature Christmas tree that reflects your favorite hobby, pastime or interest. This one's just for you!*

EXPRESSING YOURSELF is what the decorating idea here is all about. Whether your passion is crafting, cooking, playing a sport, antiquing or something else, why not celebrate it on a Christmas tree?

All you need is a miniature evergreen, a theme and a little creativity. To get you started, we've included a showcase of trimmed trees (beginning at left) featuring the themes of gardening, shopping, knitting and more. Plus, you'll find additional suggestions in the list below.

It's a wonderful way to decorate for the holidays and show off your favorite hobby at the same time. Display the tree in your home all season long—chances are, it will become quite the conversation piece!

## Need more ideas?

- *Pet Parade* If you're a fan of cats, dogs or other critters, show your enthusiasm by trimming a mini tree with pet toys, photos and a leash garland.

- *Motorcycle Mama* Born to be wild? Express your biker style and passion for the road with black and metallic ornaments. Tie a bandana to the treetop!

- *Life's a Beach* You always dream of relaxing in the sand, surf and sun...so chase away winter's chill with a "tropical paradise" tree trimmed with cocktail umbrellas, Hawaiian leis, sunglasses, etc.

- *Chef's Special* Cook up decorations that reflect your love of the kitchen. Use cookie cutters, small utensils, napkin holders and a kitchen-towel tree skirt.

- *Golfer Gal* If hitting the links is your idea of heaven, gather up golf tees, balls, score cards and more. Add tiny flags and a sun visor for the topper.

## In the Garden

Whether vegetables, fruits, herbs or flowers are your preferred plants for a garden, celebrate your hobby of working the soil. Old-world glass ornaments shaped like sunflowers, corn cobs, peas, a gardening Santa Claus and more give the basic green tree at left a pretty sheen from top to bottom. A rustic grapevine star graces the top.

**Finishing Touches:** Seed packets add whimsy tucked into the branches, and a pretty flower-print ribbon makes the ideal garland. For the base, stand the tree inside a copper-colored tub.

# Wrapped In Paper

For a creative change of pace from scrapbook pages, use your favorite paper-craft techniques to trim a tree. Make your own simple ornaments and a tree topper using precut shapes, punches, stickers, etc. Choosing festive scrapbook papers and embellishments is half the fun!

**Finishing Touches:** A piece of paper twist makes the perfect garland for a "papered" tree. Cover the sides of a small papier-mache or other box with more paper and place the base of the tree inside. Use coordinating tissue paper to fill in around the trunk.

# Noel Knitting

If your yarn and needles are never far away, cozy up to this idea. Small balls of yarn with knitting needles (cut in half with a wood bead glued to the end) add charm. Wrap wool roving around chenille stems, needle-felt the wool to secure it and bend the stems into candy canes or wreaths.

**Finishing Touches:** A purchased wooden spool garland and coordinating spool ornaments give the tree an added dimension of craftiness. You could also needle-felt wool roving into balls or gift boxes, or needle-felt simple felt cutouts. The tree's stand? A basket of yarn and wool, of course!

# Shop 'til You Drop

Love to hit the mall? Celebrate your shopping savvy and style with a tree that's just for you. The *CW* staff cut purse shapes out of card stock and covered them with fun fabric scraps. Chenille stems threaded with beads form the handles, and self-adhesive faux gemstones create the clasps.

**Finishing Touches:** This gold-tone tree stands inside a leopard-print tote. Spell "born to shop" on three separate ornaments—simply glue precut letters onto pieces of glitter foam and attach chenille stems for the hangers. Purchased high-heel ornaments add an extra touch of "diva!"

# Musical Merriment

The key to this tuneful tree is a note-worthy ribbon. Our staff attached a printed white one to a wider black one to form the garland, which stands out dramatically against the white tree. Use more of the same assembled ribbon to make a large multi-loop bow for the tree topper.

**Finishing Touches:** The musical note ornaments are actually large novelty paper clips—the back side of each clip is bent upward to form the hanger! Complete the tree with gold or silver bells, coordinating ball ornaments and an additional metallic garland.

# Give a Presentation

Let your party favors do double duty—give them a decorative look and use them as your centerpiece! Wrap a small gift (such as an ornament or chocolate candies) for each guest using elegant paper and ribbon, coordinating the colors to create a grouping. If you like, pile the gifts directly on the table…or put them on a fancy serving platter.

# Center of Attention

*Want a Christmas centerpiece that's delightfully different?*
*Think outside the flower vase with the festive ideas here.*

IT'S THE FOCAL POINT of any dining table—the decorative accent placed in the center for everyone to enjoy. And that decoration takes on even more importance during the holiday season, when you want your table to look its very best.

In this section, you'll find fun and festive centerpiece ideas that go beyond the usual vase of flowers. All are inexpensive and easy to put together yourself using materials readily available at craft stores.

From a truffle-filled tree and beautifully packaged gifts for guests to a photo holder displaying sparkling stars, these tabletop showstoppers will make any Christmas feast all the more memorable.

## Pining for Chocolate

This shimmering tree looks store-bought but is surprisingly simple to make yourself. It's low-cost, too! The *Country Woman* staff simply wrapped a white foam cone with white sparkle yarn and set it on a candlestick. Pin on wrapped truffles and invite guests to take one after dinner.

## Feather Your Nest

Tired of the same old poinsettias? Forgo those flowers for feathers! Sold in craft stores, feather stems are available in striking colors and can make a sophisticated centerpiece. Here, thin green feathers contrast with large crimson ones, which look every bit as showy as big blossoms.

# Season's Beading

"Pour" inexpensive Mardi Gras necklaces into long-stemmed glasses, and *voilà*—you have an elegant focal point for the table. You could even use your pieces of costume jewelry, or (if you're into beading) your collection of unstrung beads. Tea light candles and a few coordinating holiday ball stems enhance the festive grouping shown in the photo.

# Stars of Wonder

Craft and scrapbook stores offer a wide variety of pretty specialty papers. Why not take advantage of them for your holiday table? Here, the *CW* staff cut large stars from embossed and glitter papers. The silver and gold tones look fancy, and slipping the stars into wire photo holders creates a sparkling constellation. It's sure to make eyes light up!

# Window Wonderland

*For a breath of fresh air during the Christmas season, try these out-of-the-ordinary decorations to dress up windows in your home.*

FROM ANY VIEWPOINT, the creative accents here have "shades" of holiday spirit. Each idea is a merry way of decorating windows for Christmas!

Using the following how-to's, you can bring new growth to an empty window box...mimic Mother Nature with a flurry of snowflakes..."gift wrap" panes in elegant ribbon...enjoy scraps of festive fabrics...or display favorite photos. No matter which seasonal suggestion you choose, you'll surely take a shine to it!

## Let it Snow, Let it Snow

If you love watching snow fall—or can only imagine it because of your locale—create some frosty fun with the idea at right. Use circle punches to make white circles of three different sizes, then punch a snowflake out of the center of each. With a needle and white thread, stitch through the circles and snowflakes, attaching them along the strand of thread. Create as many of these snowflake streamers as you like to hang inside a window.

**Extra Idea:** Use colorful papers and different punches to create ornaments or stars instead of snowflakes.

## Fresh from The Box

Window boxes don't have to sit empty in cold weather—fill them for Christmas! In the photo at left, the *CW* staff arranged natural and artificial evergreen boughs, pinecones, white-painted willow twigs and berry stems. Finish with a string of white lights and a red bow.

**Extra Idea:** Combine evergreen boughs with red dogwood branches, holly, mistletoe or a bountiful selection of fruits.

# Cut from the Same Cloth

Why leave unused holiday fabric in your craft room? Use it to embellish a window! Fuse no-sew fusible web to the wrong side of an entire fabric piece following the web manufacturer's instructions, then cut out any motifs you like. Spray the wrong side of the pieces with quilter's basting spray and press them onto the glass.

**Extra Idea:** Have a window without mullion (the slats that separate the panes)? Instead of attaching several small fabric pieces as shown in the photo at left, cut a large motif in a single piece and center it on the window.

# At the Present

Wrap up a window to create a whimsical "gift package" look. In the photo at right, the *CW* staff adhered two lengths of gold mesh wire ribbon to the trim on the exterior of a window to resemble a be-ribboned box. Tie a third piece into a large bow and attach it to the center.

**Extra Idea:** Repeat the same ribbon decoration on the *inside* of your window so you can enjoy the same adornment when indoors as well.

# *Photo Opportunity*

If you have access to a computer with an inkjet printer, then you can turn your favorite holiday snapshots into fun window clings. Just print each photo on clear window decal paper (available at office supply stores) following the paper manufacturer's instructions. Remove the backing from the printed photo and place it on your window for all to see and enjoy.

**Extra Idea:** Use a photocopier to transfer your child's artwork onto the window decal paper to create a personal art display.

## *Tips!*

### When Making Window Clings With Photos:

- For best results, use pictures that have very saturated colors and simple designs.

- To add visual interest, create clings of different sizes as shown in the photo at left. Or, experiment with border and corner designs to decorate just the window's edges.

- Simple designs can be cut out and enhanced by outlining them with dimensional paint for a stained-glass look. Apply the paint to the side that does not face the glass.

- The window clings can be reused. Just save the backing, place the photos back on it after Christmas and store them for next year.

# Nutcracker Ballet Party

*Invite kids for a fanciful time featuring yummy food*
*and fun activities based on the classic Christmastime story.*

THE SUGAR PLUM FAIRY, Land of Sweets, Mouse King, Snow Queen…it all sets the stage for a magically fun Christmas party. The theme? *The Nutcracker Ballet!*

The enchantment and beauty of that classic ballet have made it an annual tradition during the holiday season. And it's easy to re-create that wonder and delight in your own home as a merry event for kids.

Charm the aspiring ballerinas and dashing princes on your guest list with a special Nutcracker-themed menu (recipes start on page 22) and suggestions for "Easy Party Activities" on page 25.

Planning to bring kids to see an actual performance of the ballet? Use these ideas to host an after-party!

## Party Menu

*Sugar Plum Fairy Cupcakes*

**2.** Fill paper-lined muffin cups two-thirds full. Bake at 350° for 18-22 minutes or until a toothpick inserted in the center comes out clean. Cool for 10 minutes before removing from pan to a wire rack to cool completely.

**3.** Cut a small hole in the corner of a pastry or plastic bag; insert a very small tip. Fill with jam. Push the tip through the top to fill each cupcake.

**4.** For frosting, combine the sugar, egg whites, water and cream of tartar in a large heavy saucepan over low heat. With a hand mixer, beat on low speed for 1 minute. Continue beating on low over low heat until frosting reaches 160°, about 8-10 minutes. Pour into a large bowl; add vanilla. Beat on high until stiff peaks form, about 7 minutes.

**5.** Pipe frosting over cupcakes; sprinkle with glitter and coarse sugar. **Yield:** 16 cupcakes.

**Editor's Note:** Edible glitter is available from Wilton Industries. Call 1-800/794-5866 or visit *www.wilton.com.*

## Pink Party Punch

*—Carol Garnett, Bellevue, Washington*

  2 bottles (46 ounces *each*) white grape juice, chilled
  1 bottle (48 ounces) cranberry juice, chilled
  2 cans (12 ounces *each*) frozen lemonade concentrate, thawed
  1 bottle (1 liter) club soda, chilled
  1 pint lemon sherbet

**1.** In two pitchers, combine juices and lemonade concentrate; refrigerate until serving.

**2.** Just before serving, stir in club soda and top with scoops of sherbet. **Yield:** 32 servings (6 quarts).

## Sugar Plum Fairy Cupcakes

*—Taste of Home Test Kitchen*

  1/2 cup butter, softened
1-1/2 cups sugar
  4 egg whites
  2 teaspoons vanilla extract
  2 cups all-purpose flour
  1 teaspoon baking powder
1/2 teaspoon baking soda
1/4 teaspoon salt
1-1/3 cups buttermilk
  1 cup plum jam
FROSTING:
  1 cup sugar
  2 egg whites
1/4 cup water
1/4 teaspoon cream of tartar
  1 teaspoon vanilla extract
Edible glitter and coarse sugar

**1.** In a large bowl, cream butter and sugar until light and fluffy. Add egg whites, one at a time, beating well after each addition. Beat in vanilla. Combine the flour, baking powder, baking soda and salt; add to the creamed mixture alternately with buttermilk, beating well after each addition.

*Pink Party Punch*

❄ *Special Feature* ❄

*Mini Barbecued Ham Sandwiches*
*Mouse King Cheese Soup*

1/2 cup butter
3/4 cup all-purpose flour
1 teaspoon salt
3 quarts 2% milk
1-1/3 cups reduced-sodium chicken broth
1 package (8 ounces) process cheese (Velveeta), shredded
1-1/2 cups (6 ounces) shredded cheddar cheese

In a Dutch oven, saute the carrots, celery, onion and green pepper in butter until tender. Stir in flour and salt until blended; gradually add milk and broth. Bring to a boil; cook and stir for 2 minutes or until thickened. Reduce heat to low; stir in cheeses until melted. **Yield:** 12 servings (3 quarts).

## Toy Soldier Apple Salad

—*Susan Falk, Eastpointe, Michigan*

2 large green apples, chopped
2 large red apples, chopped
1/2 cup chopped walnuts
1/4 cup flaked coconut
1/4 cup raisins
1 cup vanilla yogurt
1 tablespoon honey
1/2 teaspoon ground cinnamon

In a large bowl, combine the first five ingredients. In a small bowl, whisk the yogurt, honey and cinnamon until blended. Pour over apple mixture; toss to coat. Refrigerate until serving. **Yield:** 9 servings.

*Toy Soldier Apple Salad*

## Mini Barbecued Ham Sandwiches

—*Susanne Roupe, East Fairfield, Vermont*

1 cup chili sauce
1/2 cup water
2 tablespoons sugar
2 tablespoons cider vinegar
1 tablespoon Worcestershire sauce
1 teaspoon onion powder
1 pound fully cooked ham, very thinly sliced
24 dinner rolls, split

In a large saucepan, combine the first six ingredients. Bring to a boil. Reduce heat; simmer, uncovered, for 6-8 minutes or until slightly thickened. Stir in ham; heat through. Serve on rolls. **Yield:** 2 dozen.

## Mouse King Cheese Soup

—*Sharon Delaney-Chronis, South Milwaukee, Wisconsin*

4 medium carrots, chopped
2 celery ribs, chopped
1 large onion, chopped
1 medium green pepper, chopped

*Nutcracker Butter Cookies*

**3.** For icing, in a large bowl, combine the confectioners' sugar, water and meringue powder; beat on low speed just until combined. Beat on high for 4-5 minutes or until stiff peaks form. Tint icing as desired with food coloring. (Keep unused icing covered at all times with a damp cloth. If necessary, beat again on high speed to restore texture.)

**4.** Using pastry bags and small round tips, decorate cookies as desired. Let dry at room temperature for several hours or until firm. Store in an airtight container. **Yield:** 1 dozen.

## Italian Puff Pastry Twists
*—Taste of Home Test Kitchen*

    1/4 cup butter, melted
      1 garlic clove, minced
      1 teaspoon Italian seasoning
      1 package (17.3 ounces) frozen puff pastry, thawed
    1/4 cup grated Parmesan cheese

**1.** In a small bowl, combine the butter, garlic and Italian seasoning; set aside.

**2.** On a lightly floured surface, roll each pastry sheet into a 12-in. x 10-in. rectangle; cut each widthwise into 1-in. strips.

**3.** Twist each strip two to three times; place on greased baking sheets. Brush with butter mixture; sprinkle with cheese. Bake at 400° for 8-12 minutes or until golden brown. **Yield:** 2 dozen.

*Italian Puff Pastry Twists*

## Nutcracker Butter Cookies
*—Dorothy Jennings, Waterloo, Iowa*

    1/2 cup butter, softened
    3/4 cup sugar
      1 egg
    3/4 teaspoon vanilla extract
    1-3/4 cups all-purpose flour
    1/2 teaspoon baking powder
    1/4 teaspoon salt
    ROYAL ICING:
      4 cups confectioners' sugar
      6 tablespoons water
      3 tablespoons meringue powder
    Paste food coloring of your choice

**1.** In a small bowl, cream butter and sugar until light and fluffy. Beat in egg and vanilla. Combine flour, baking powder and salt; gradually add to creamed mixture and mix well. Cover and refrigerate for 1 hour or until easy to handle.

**2.** On a lightly floured surface, roll out to 1/8-in. thickness. Cut with a 6-in. nutcracker cookie cutter. Place 2 in. apart on ungreased baking sheets. Bake at 350° for 8-10 minutes or until lightly browned. Cool on wire racks.

✳ *Special Feature* ✳

# EASY PARTY ACTIVITIES

**Let the kids play dress-up.** Check discount stores for inexpensive play clothes and let the girls become prima ballerinas with tutus, fairy wings and tiaras. Boys will have fun as nutcracker princes with crowns and foam toy swords.

**Get them dancing.** The popular music composed by Tchaikovsky for *The Nutcracker Ballet* is perfect. Clear a space as the "stage" for dancing and pirouetting. Play a video of the ballet performance on your TV, or pop in the CD.

**Set up a crafts table.** Using child-safe scissors or paper punches, kids can cut snowflakes and flowers from colorful construction paper. Or, offer them holiday stickers, crayons, washable markers and Christmas coloring books.

**Share an illustrated book.** Tchaikovsky's *The Nutcracker Ballet* was loosely based on a tale by E.T.A. Hoffman. Many kid-friendly versions of *The Nutcracker* are available in libraries, in bookstores and online. Gather kids around a colorful book and read the whimsical story.

# Holiday
## RECIPES

*Christmastime calls for foods that are extra special...
and you'll find all kinds in this appetizing chapter.*

*Veggie Couscous Quiche*

# Veggie Couscous Quiche

*Tomato, green onions and broccoli bring red and green color to this sunrise specialty, giving it Christmasy flair. It also gets a taste twist from nutmeg. —Julie Kirkpatrick, Billings, Montana*

    1 egg
    1/2 teaspoon onion salt
    2 cups cooked couscous, cooled
    1/4 cup shredded Swiss cheese
FILLING:
    4 eggs
    1 cup half-and-half cream
    4 cups frozen broccoli florets, thawed
    1 can (6 ounces) sliced mushrooms, drained
    1 cup (4 ounces) shredded Swiss cheese, *divided*
    1/4 teaspoon ground nutmeg
    1 plum tomato, finely chopped
    2 green onions, chopped

**1.** In a small bowl, whisk egg and onion salt. Add couscous and cheese; stir until blended. Press onto the bottom and up the sides of a greased 9-in. deep-dish pie plate. Bake at 350° for 5 minutes.

**2.** In a large bowl, whisk eggs and cream. Stir in the broccoli, mushrooms, 1/2 cup cheese and nutmeg. Pour into crust. Bake for 45-55 minutes or until a knife inserted near the center comes out clean.

**3.** Sprinkle with tomato, onions and remaining cheese. Bake 3-5 minutes longer or until cheese is melted. Let stand for 10 minutes before cutting. **Yield:** 6 servings.

# Apple-Pecan Cinnamon Rolls

*With cream cheese frosting on top, these treats are sure to become a holiday "must" at your house. Using the bread machine keeps preparation easy. —Sherri Emerson, Penn Yan, New York*

    1 cup warm milk (70° to 80°)
    2 eggs
    1/3 cup butter, melted
    1/2 cup sugar
    1 teaspoon salt
    4-1/2 cups bread flour
    2-1/2 teaspoons bread machine yeast
FILLING:
    3 tablespoons butter, melted
    1 cup finely chopped peeled apples
    3/4 cup packed brown sugar
    1/3 cup chopped pecans

    2-1/2 teaspoons ground cinnamon
ICING:
    1-1/2 cups confectioners' sugar
    1 package (3 ounces) cream cheese, softened
    1/4 cup butter, softened
    1/2 teaspoon vanilla extract
    1/8 teaspoon salt

**1.** In bread machine pan, place the first seven ingredients in order suggested by manufacturer. Select dough setting (check dough after 5 minutes of mixing; add 1 to 2 tablespoons of water or flour if needed). When cycle is completed, turn dough onto a well-floured surface.

**2.** Roll into a 21-in. x 16-in. rectangle; brush with butter. Combine the apples, brown sugar, pecans and cinnamon; spoon over dough to within 1/2 in. of edges. Roll up jelly-roll style, starting with a long side; pinch seam to seal. Cut into 1-3/4-in. slices.

**3.** Place cut side down in a greased 13-in. x 9-in. baking dish. Cover and let rise until nearly doubled, about 30 minutes. Bake at 325° for 25-30 minutes or until golden brown.

**4.** In a small bowl, beat the icing ingredients. Spread over warm rolls. **Yield:** 12 servings.

**Editor's Note:** We recommend you do not use a bread machine's time-delay feature for this recipe.

*Apple-Pecan Cinnamon Rolls*

# Blueberry Waffles

*These light, tender homemade waffles are just bursting with juicy blueberries—and are topped with a blueberry sauce, too!*
—Devyn Weakley, Howard, Kansas

      2 cups all-purpose flour
2-1/4 teaspoons baking powder
      1/2 teaspoon salt
1-2/3 cups milk
      3 eggs, *separated*
      1/4 cup butter, melted
      2/3 cup fresh *or* frozen blueberries
SAUCE:
1-1/2 cups fresh *or* frozen blueberries
      1/2 cup orange juice, *divided*
      3 tablespoons honey
      1 tablespoon cornstarch

**1.** In a large bowl, combine the flour, baking powder and salt. Whisk the milk, egg yolks and butter; stir into dry ingredients just until moistened. Fold in blueberries.

**2.** In a small bowl, beat egg whites until stiff peaks form; fold into batter. Bake in a preheated waffle iron according to manufacturer's directions until golden brown.

**3.** Meanwhile, in a small saucepan, combine the blueberries, 1/4 cup orange juice and honey. Bring to a boil. Combine cornstarch and remaining orange juice until smooth; gradually stir into the blueberry mixture. Bring to a boil; cook and stir for 2 minutes or until thickened. Serve warm with waffles. **Yield:** 12 waffles (1-1/3 cups sauce).

**Editor's Note:** If using frozen blueberries, use without thawing to avoid discoloring the batter.

*Blueberry Waffles*

# Sweet Orange Croissant Pudding

*Time-crunched cooks are sure to appreciate the make-ahead convenience of this delightful dish. Feel free to replace the orange marmalade with any jam or jelly that suits your taste.*
—Mary Gabriel, Las Vegas, Nevada

      4 croissants, split
      1 cup orange marmalade, *divided*
      3 eggs
1-1/4 cups milk
      1 cup heavy whipping cream
      1/2 cup sugar
      1 teaspoon grated orange peel, optional
      1/2 teaspoon almond extract

**1.** Spread croissant bottoms with 3 tablespoons marmalade; replace tops. Cut each croissant into five slices; place in a greased 11-in. x 7-in. baking dish.

**2.** In a large bowl, whisk the eggs, milk, cream, sugar, orange peel if desired and extract; pour over croissants. Cover and refrigerate overnight.

**3.** Remove from the refrigerator 30 minutes before baking. Place dish in a larger baking dish. Fill larger dish with 1 in. of boiling water.

**4.** Bake, uncovered, at 350° for 40-45 minutes or until a knife inserted near the center comes out clean.

**5.** Remove pan from the water bath; cool on a wire rack for 10 minutes. Brush remaining marmalade over the top. Cut and serve warm. **Yield:** 8 servings.

# Bacon-Ranch Mini Loaves

*Need to round out your morning menu on Christmas...or anytime at all? Try these savory miniature loaves that bake up tender and golden brown. Slices are wonderful alongside vegetable omelets, breakfast bakes, frittatas or any favorite egg dish.*
—Brandon Norton, Auburn, Kentucky

      1/2 pound bacon strips, diced
      1 cup chopped green onions
      3 cups all-purpose flour
      2 tablespoons sugar
      2 teaspoons baking powder
      2 teaspoons ranch salad dressing mix
1-1/2 teaspoons garlic powder
      1 teaspoon baking soda
      1 teaspoon pepper
      2 eggs
1-1/2 cups 2% milk
      3 tablespoons butter, melted
      2 cups (8 ounces) shredded sharp cheddar cheese

**1.** In a large skillet, cook bacon over medium heat until crisp. Using a slotted spoon, remove to paper towels. Drain, reserving 1 tablespoon drippings. Saute onions in reserved drippings until tender; cool.

**2.** In a large bowl, combine the flour, sugar, baking powder, dressing mix, garlic powder, baking soda and pepper. In a small bowl, whisk the eggs, milk and butter. Stir into dry ingredients just until moistened. Fold in the cheese, bacon and onions.

**3.** Transfer to four greased 5-3/4-in. x 3-in. x 2-in. loaf pans. Bake at 350° for 30-35 minutes or until a toothpick inserted near the center comes out clean. Cool for 10 minutes before removing loaves from pans to wire racks. **Yield:** 4 mini loaves (6 slices each).

**Editor's Note:** Bread can be baked in two greased 8-in. x 4-in. loaf pans for 35-40 minutes.

# Gouda Turkey Frittata

*You'll want to enjoy this cheesy, filling egg skillet not only for breakfast, but also for dinner. The hearty frittata is a great way to use up turkey leftovers.* —Nella Parker, Hersey, Michigan

    1 cup diced zucchini
    2 shallots, finely chopped
    1 tablespoon olive oil
    1 tablespoon butter
    4 eggs
    2 tablespoons water
    1 cup finely chopped cooked turkey
1-1/2 teaspoons minced fresh tarragon
  1/4 teaspoon salt
  1/4 teaspoon pepper
  1/2 cup shredded Gouda cheese

**1.** In a 10-in. ovenproof skillet, saute zucchini and shallots in oil and butter until tender.

**2.** In a small bowl, whisk eggs and water; stir in turkey and seasonings. Pour egg mixture into skillet; cover and cook over medium-low heat for 8-10 minutes or until eggs are nearly set.

**3.** Uncover skillet; sprinkle with cheese. Broil 6 in. from the heat for 2-3 minutes or until eggs are completely set. Cut into wedges. **Yield:** 6 servings.

# Apple Sausage Puffs

*I love serving these tender little puffs when I entertain during the holiday season. No one is able to resist them, and I need just four basic ingredients to prepare the simple recipe.* —Veronica Johnson, Jefferson City, Missouri

1 pound bulk pork sausage
1 medium apple, finely chopped
3 ounces cream cheese, softened
3 tubes (8 ounces *each*) refrigerated crescent rolls

**1.** In a large skillet, cook sausage and apple over medium heat until meat is no longer pink; drain. Stir in cream cheese.

**2.** Unroll one tube of crescent dough; separate into eight triangles. Place 1 tablespoon filling on the long side of each triangle. Roll up starting with a long side; pinch seams to seal.

*Apple Sausage Puffs*

**3.** Place point side down 2 in. apart on a greased baking sheet. Repeat with remaining crescent dough and filling. Bake at 375° for 10-12 minutes or until golden brown. Serve warm. **Yield:** 2 dozen.

# Chilled Fruit Cups

*Our Christmas meal always began with this refreshing, colorful cup that combines seven different fruits. You could even serve it as a light summer dessert with a scoop of lime sherbet.* —Janet Wood, Windham, New Hampshire

1/2 cup sugar
1/2 cup water
  2 medium grapefruit, cut into sections
  2 medium navel oranges, cut into sections
1/4 cup lemon juice
  2 cups halved fresh strawberries
  1 medium red apple, cut into 1/2-inch cubes
  1 medium pear, cut into 1/2-inch cubes
  1 medium banana, halved lengthwise and thinly sliced
  1 cup halved green grapes

**1.** In a small saucepan, bring the sugar and water to a boil. Reduce heat; simmer for 5 minutes. Cool. In a large bowl, combine the grapefruit, oranges, lemon juice and sugar mixture. Cover and refrigerate for 8 hours or overnight.

**2.** Stir in the strawberries, apple, pear, banana and grapes. Cover and refrigerate for 1 hour. Spoon into dessert cups. **Yield:** 10 servings.

*Chorizo Tomato Strata*

## Chorizo Tomato Strata

*With chorizo sausage, this oven-baked dish is a satisfying main course for any special breakfast. The seasonings blend to create a tantalizing taste everyone at your table will remember.*
*—Donna Cowley, Mount Morris, Illinois*

1/2 pound uncooked chorizo
1 cup (4 ounces) shredded Gruyere cheese, *divided*
1/4 cup minced fresh cilantro
1 garlic clove, halved
1 loaf (1/2 pound) day-old French bread, cut into
   1-inch slices
2 large tomatoes, sliced
8 eggs
2 cups milk
3/4 teaspoon salt
3/4 teaspoon pepper
1/2 teaspoon onion powder
1/4 teaspoon crushed red pepper flakes

**1.** Crumble chorizo into a small skillet; cook and stir over medium heat until fully cooked. Drain. Stir in 1/3 cup cheese and cilantro.

**2.** Rub the cut side of garlic clove over bread slices; discard garlic. Place bread in a greased 13-in. x 9-in. baking dish. Top with tomatoes, meat mixture and remaining cheese.

**3.** In a large bowl, whisk the eggs, milk, salt, pepper, onion powder and pepper flakes. Pour over casserole.

**4.** Bake, uncovered, at 350° for 35-45 minutes or until a knife inserted near the center comes out clean (cover loosely with foil if top browns too quickly). Let stand for 10 minutes before cutting. **Yield:** 12 servings.

## Chai Tea

*Warm up a chilly December morning—or any day at all—with this inviting tea. The spices really come through, and it's even more delicious when stirred with a cinnamon stick.*
*—Kelly Pacowta, Danbury, Connecticut*

4 whole cloves
2 whole peppercorns
4 individual tea bags
4 teaspoons sugar
1/4 teaspoon ground ginger
1 cinnamon stick (3 inches)
2-1/2 cups boiling water
2 cups milk

**1.** Place the cloves and peppercorns in a large bowl; with the end of a wooden spoon handle, crush the spices until the aromas are released.

**2.** Add the tea bags, sugar, ginger, cinnamon stick and boiling water. Cover and steep for 6 minutes. Meanwhile, in a small saucepan, heat the milk.

**3.** Strain tea, discarding spices and tea bags. Stir in hot milk. Pour into mugs. **Yield:** 4 servings.

## Cheese-Filled Lemon Coffee Cake

*Lemon lovers will find this rich, glazed coffee cake absolutely scrumptious. The cream cheese in the middle is a wonderful surprise and nicely complements the tart citrus flavor.*
*—Tessa Mabe, Toledo, Oregon*

1/3 cup butter, softened
1-1/2 cups sugar, *divided*
1 egg
1/2 cup lemon juice
2 tablespoons grated lemon peel
2 cups all-purpose flour
2 teaspoons baking powder
1/2 teaspoon salt
1/2 cup milk
5 ounces cream cheese, softened
GLAZE:
1/2 cup confectioners' sugar
4-1/2 teaspoons butter, melted
4-1/2 teaspoons lemon juice
1/4 teaspoon grated lemon peel

**1.** In a large bowl, beat the butter and 1 cup sugar until crumbly, about 2 minutes. Add egg; mix well. Stir in lemon juice and lemon peel.

**2.** Combine the flour, baking powder and salt; add to the creamed mixture alternately with the milk, beating well after each addition.

**3.** Pour half of the batter into a greased and floured 8-in. fluted tube pan. In a small bowl, combine the cream cheese and remaining sugar; spoon over the batter. Top with the remaining batter.

**4.** Bake at 350° for 40-45 minutes or until a toothpick inserted near the center comes out clean. Cool for 10 minutes before removing from pan to a wire rack to cool completely.

**5.** In a small bowl, combine glaze ingredients. Drizzle over cake. Refrigerate leftovers. **Yield:** 6 servings.

Cheese-Filled Lemon Coffee Cake
Chai Tea

*Ribbon Nut Bread*

# Ribbon Nut Bread

*With lemon, walnuts and a center of sweetened cream cheese, this lovely loaf is a tempting holiday treat. I like making an extra one to wrap up and give as a gift to a friend or neighbor.*
—*Linda Evancoe-Coble, Leola, Pennsylvania*

    1 package (8 ounces) cream cheese, softened
1/3 cup sugar
    1 egg
BATTER:
    2 cups all-purpose flour
1/3 cup sugar
1/3 cup packed brown sugar
    1 teaspoon baking soda
1/2 teaspoon salt
    2 eggs
1/2 cup milk
1/2 cup canola oil
    1 teaspoon grated lemon peel
    1 cup chopped walnuts

**1.** For filling, in a small bowl, beat cream cheese and sugar. Beat in egg; set aside.

**2.** In a large bowl, combine the flour, sugars, baking soda and salt. Whisk the eggs, milk, oil and lemon peel; stir into dry ingredients just until moistened. Fold in walnuts.

**3.** Spoon 1 cup batter into a greased 9-in. x 5-in. loaf pan. Spread filling evenly over batter. Top with remaining batter, carefully spreading to cover.

**4.** Bake at 350° for 55-60 minutes or until a toothpick inserted near the center comes out clean. Cool for 10 minutes before removing from pan to a wire rack. Store in the refrigerator. **Yield:** 1 loaf (16 slices).

# Upside-Down Onion Bread

*This rich, savory bread is loaded with cheddar cheese, chopped sweet onion and crumbled bacon. The thick wedges are delicious served alongside your entree...or even used for sandwiches.*
—*Mary Leverette, Columbia, South Carolina*

    1 large sweet onion, chopped
    1 tablespoon olive oil
    1 tablespoon butter
3/4 teaspoon minced fresh thyme
    3 cups all-purpose flour
    3 teaspoons baking powder
    3 teaspoons sugar
    1 teaspoon salt
    1 teaspoon pepper
    1 cup cold butter
    1 cup heavy whipping cream
1-1/2 cups (6 ounces) shredded sharp cheddar cheese
1/2 cup crumbled cooked bacon

**1.** In a large skillet over low heat, cook the onion in the oil and butter for 50 minutes or until golden brown, stirring occasionally. Transfer to a greased 9-in. deep-dish pie plate; sprinkle with the thyme.

**2.** In a large bowl, combine the flour, baking powder, sugar, salt and pepper. Cut in butter until mixture resembles coarse crumbs. Stir in cream just until moistened. Fold in cheese and bacon. Turn onto a lightly floured surface; knead 8-10 times. Pat or roll into a 9-in. circle. Carefully place over onions.

**3.** Bake at 400° for 30-35 minutes or until golden brown. Immediately invert onto a large serving platter. Cool slightly; serve warm. **Yield:** 1 loaf (10 wedges).

*Upside-Down Onion Bread*

# Almond-Filled Breakfast Rolls

*A sweet, buttery almond filling is rolled into these homespun treats. Topped with more nuts, they're an irresistible addition to any breakfast spread.* —Ann Nace, Perkasie, Pennsylvania

```
3-1/2 cups all-purpose flour
  1/4 cup plus 1 tablespoon sugar, divided
  3/4 teaspoon salt
  1/2 cup cold butter
    1 package (1/4 ounce) active dry yeast
  1/4 cup warm milk (110° to 115°)
    1 cup warm heavy whipping cream (110° to 115°)
    3 egg yolks, beaten
ALMOND FILLING:
  3/4 cup almond cake and pastry filling
  1/4 cup butter, softened
EGG WASH:
    1 egg, beaten
  1/2 cup slivered almonds
```

**1.** In a large bowl, combine the flour, 1/4 cup sugar and salt. Cut in butter until crumbly. In a small bowl, dissolve yeast in warm milk. Add the remaining sugar; let stand for 5 minutes. Add cream and egg yolks; mix well. Stir into dry ingredients; mix well. Do not knead. Cover and refrigerate overnight.

**2.** For filling, in a small bowl, beat almond paste and butter until smooth. Punch dough down; turn onto a lightly floured surface. Divide in half. Roll each portion into a 12-in. square. Spread filling to within 1/2 in. of edges. Roll up jelly-roll style; pinch seams to seal. Cut each into 14 rolls. Place rolls, cut-side up, on greased baking sheets. Cover and let rise in a warm place for 45 minutes (dough will not double).

**3.** Brush with egg; sprinkle with almonds. Bake at 375° for 15-20 minutes or until golden. Remove from pans to wire racks to cool. **Yield:** 28 rolls.

**Editor's Note:** This recipe was tested with Solo brand cake and pastry filling. Look for it in the baking aisle.

*Almond-Filled Breakfast Rolls*

# Multigrain Bread

*This healthful loaf loaded with whole grains couldn't be much easier to make—you just combine the ingredients in a bread machine and let it do the rest of the work for you! Stack slices high with leftover turkey or ham from your special meals.* —Ruth Skafte, Fort St. John, British Columbia

```
1-1/3 cups water (70° to 80°)
    2 tablespoons shortening
    2 tablespoons honey
  1/2 cup seven-grain cereal
  1/3 cup flaxseed
    2 tablespoons nonfat dry milk powder
    2 tablespoons unsalted sunflower kernels
    1 tablespoon sesame seeds
    1 teaspoon salt
    2 cups all-purpose flour
    1 cup whole wheat flour
    1 package (1/4 ounce) active dry yeast
```

In bread machine pan, place all the ingredients in the order suggested by manufacturer. Select basic bread setting. Choose crust color and loaf size if available. Bake according to bread machine directions (check dough after 5 minutes of mixing; add 1 to 2 tablespoons of water or flour if needed). **Yield:** 1 loaf (2 pounds, 16 slices).

# Pineapple Coffee Cake

*Moist and fruity, this coffee cake combines pineapple bits with coconut and a hint of honey. It's a wonderful choice for brunch, as an afternoon treat with tea or even after dinner with coffee.* —Janice Whalen, Baldwinville, Massachusetts

```
    1 can (8 ounces) crushed pineapple
1-1/2 cups all-purpose flour
  1/2 cup sugar
    2 teaspoons baking powder
  1/2 teaspoon salt
  1/2 teaspoon ground mace
    1 egg, beaten
  1/4 cup canola oil
  1/4 cup milk
    3 tablespoons butter, softened
  1/3 cup honey
  1/2 cup crushed cornflakes
  1/4 cup flaked coconut
```

**1.** Drain the pineapple, reserving juice. Set pineapple aside. In a large bowl, combine the flour, sugar, baking powder, salt and mace. In a small bowl, combine the egg, oil, milk and reserved pineapple juice. Stir into the dry ingredients just until moistened.

**2.** Transfer to a greased 9-in. round baking pan. In a small bowl, beat butter and honey until well blended. Fold in the cornflakes, coconut and reserved pineapple. Gently spread over batter.

**3.** Bake at 400° for 20-25 minutes or until a toothpick inserted near the center comes out clean. Place on a wire rack. **Yield:** 8 servings.

# Honey Potato Rolls

*Made with mashed potatoes, these golden-brown goodies will complement just about any meal. I always included them as part of my holiday menu when my daughters were growing up, and now the girls carry on the tradition with their own families.*
—Myrna Wolfswinkel, Sheldon, Iowa

    1 package (1/4 ounce) active dry yeast
1-1/2 cups warm water (110° to 115°)
    1 cup mashed potatoes (without added milk and
      butter)
  2/3 cup butter, softened
  2/3 cup honey
    2 eggs
1-1/2 teaspoons salt
    4 to 4-1/2 cups all-purpose flour
    2 cups whole wheat flour
    2 tablespoons butter, melted

**1.** In a large bowl, dissolve yeast in warm water. Add the mashed potatoes, butter, honey, eggs, salt and 2 cups all-purpose flour; beat until smooth. Stir in whole wheat flour and enough remaining all-purpose flour to form a soft dough.

**2.** Turn dough onto a floured surface; knead until smooth and elastic, about 6-8 minutes. Place in a greased bowl, turning once to grease the top. Cover and refrigerate for 8 hours or overnight.

**3.** Punch down dough. Turn onto a lightly floured surface; divide into 40 pieces. Shape each piece into a ball. Divide between two greased 13-in. x 9-in. baking pans. Cover and let rise in a warm place until doubled, about 1-1/2 hours.

**4.** Bake at 375° for 15-20 minutes or until golden brown; brush with melted butter. **Yield:** about 3 dozen.

# Buttery Herb Christmas Tree

*Your guests will be "pining" for this pull-apart treat shaped like a festive evergreen. Each roll is tender, flaky and flavored with a homemade herb butter sure to make mouths water. If you like, add "decorations" to the tree using seasonings or veggies.*
—Kathryn Pollock, Tropic, Utah

    1 package (1/4 ounce) active dry yeast
    2 tablespoons warm water (110° to 115°)
1/2 cup warm 2% milk (110° to 115°)
1/4 cup butter, softened
    1 egg
    2 tablespoons sugar
    1 teaspoon salt
2-1/2 to 3 cups all-purpose flour
HERB BUTTER:
1/4 cup butter, softened
    1 small garlic clove, minced
1/2 teaspoon dried basil
1/2 teaspoon dried oregano
1/4 teaspoon dried minced onion
Dash cayenne pepper
    1 tablespoon water
    1 teaspoon sesame seeds

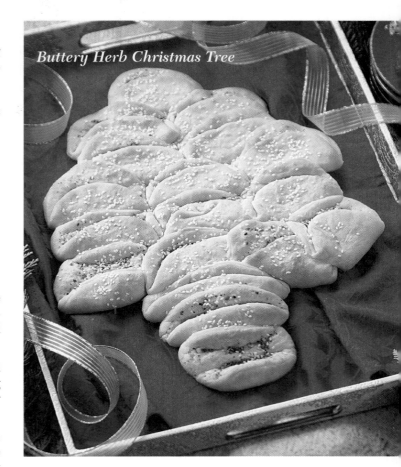

Buttery Herb Christmas Tree

**1.** In a large bowl, dissolve yeast in warm water. Add the milk, butter, egg, sugar, salt and 1-1/2 cups flour. Beat until smooth. Stir in enough remaining flour to form a firm dough.

**2.** Turn onto a lightly floured surface; knead until smooth and elastic, about 6-8 minutes. Place in a greased bowl, turning once to grease the top. Cover and let rise in a warm place until doubled, about 1 hour.

**3.** Punch dough down. Turn onto a lightly floured surface. Roll out dough to 1/8-in. thickness; cut out into seventeen 3-1/2-in. circles.

**4.** For herb butter, combine the butter, garlic, basil, oregano, onion and cayenne. Set aside 1 teaspoon herb butter. Spread the remaining herb butter over dough circles to within 1/2 in. of edges. Using the dull edge of a table knife, make an off-center crease in each roll. Fold along crease.

**5.** To form tree, place one roll near the top center of a greased 15-in. x 10-in. x 1-in. baking pan. Arrange 14 rolls overlapping slightly, forming a tree shape. Use water to moisten dough where it overlaps.

**6.** For trunk, place remaining rolls on bottom of tree. Cover and let rise until doubled, about 40 minutes.

**7.** In microwave, melt the reserved butter mixture. Brush over the rolls; sprinkle with sesame seeds. Bake at 350° for 15-20 minutes or until golden brown. Serve rolls warm. **Yield:** 1 tree (17 rolls).

*Herb Quick Bread*

# Herb Quick Bread

*This savory bread recipe yields three mini loaves and is so versatile—you can mix up different herbs and cheeses to suit your family's taste.* —Karen Paumen, Annandale, Minnesota

2-1/4 cups all-purpose flour
   2 ounces provolone cheese, shredded
1/2 cup grated Parmesan cheese
1/4 cup minced fresh parsley
   1 teaspoon baking powder
   1 teaspoon sugar
   1 teaspoon salt
   1 teaspoon pepper
3/4 teaspoon dried thyme
1/2 teaspoon baking soda
1/2 teaspoon dried savory
   2 eggs
1-1/4 cups buttermilk
   3 tablespoons canola oil

**1.** In a large bowl, combine the first 11 ingredients. In a small bowl, whisk the eggs, buttermilk and oil. Stir into dry ingredients just until moistened.

**2.** Transfer to three greased 5-3/4-in. x 3-in. x 2-in. loaf pans. Bake at 350° for 25-30 minutes or until a toothpick inserted near the center comes out clean. Cool for 10 minutes before removing from the pans to wire racks. **Yield:** 3 mini loaves (6 slices each).

# Pineapple Tea Rings

*Topped with icing, cherries and nuts, this pineapple-filled treat is sure to get attention on a holiday table. And the flavor won't disappoint!* —Barbara McCalley, Allison Park, Pennsylvania

   2 packages (1/4 ounce *each*) active dry yeast
1/4 cup warm water (110° to 115°)
   1 cup warm 2% milk (110° to 115°)
1/2 cup sugar
1/4 cup shortening
   2 eggs
   1 teaspoon salt
5-1/2 to 6 cups all-purpose flour
   6 tablespoons brown sugar
   2 teaspoons ground cinnamon
FILLING:
   1 can (20 ounces) unsweetened crushed pineapple, drained
3/4 cup sugar
   1 tablespoon cornstarch
1/2 cup raisins
1/4 cup butter, melted
DRIZZLE:
   1 cup confectioners' sugar
   1 tablespoon butter, melted
   4 teaspoons 2% milk
1/2 teaspoon vanilla extract
Maraschino cherries and chopped nuts, optional

**1.** In a large bowl, dissolve the yeast in warm water. Add the warm milk, sugar, shortening, eggs, salt and 4-1/2 cups flour. Beat until smooth. Stir in enough remaining flour to form a stiff dough.

**2.** Turn onto a lightly floured surface; knead until smooth and elastic, about 5-6 minutes. Place in a greased bowl, turning once to grease top. Cover and let rise in a warm place until doubled, about 1 hour.

**3.** Meanwhile, combine brown sugar and cinnamon; set aside. In a small saucepan, combine the pineapple, sugar and cornstarch. Cook, uncovered, over medium heat until thickened. Stir in raisins; cool.

**4.** Punch dough down; turn onto a lightly floured surface. Divide in half. Roll one portion into a 20-in. x 12-in. rectangle. Brush with 2 tablespoons melted butter. Spread with 1 cup pineapple filling to within 1 in. of edges. Sprinkle with 3 tablespoons brown sugar mixture. Roll up jelly-roll style, starting with a long side. Pinch seam to seal. Place seam side down on a greased baking sheet; pinch ends together to form a ring.

**5.** With scissors, cut from outside edge to two-thirds of the way toward center of ring at 1-in. intervals. Separate strips slightly, alternating strips towards the inside and outside of the ring. Twist to allow filling to show.

**6.** Repeat with the remaining dough, melted butter and pineapple filling. Cover and let rise in a warm place until doubled, about 1 hour.

**7.** Bake at 350° for 20-25 minutes or until golden brown. Remove from pan to a wire rack to cool.

**8.** Combine the confectioners' sugar, butter, milk and vanilla; beat until smooth. Drizzle over tea rings. Decorate with cherries and nuts. **Yield:** 2 rings (16 slices each).

Pineapple Tea Rings

# Sugar Plum Scones

*Dried plums and a sprinkling of coarse sugar make these treats delightfully Christmasy. Spread them with butter, cream cheese or preserves.* —Julie McQuiston, Bradenton, Florida

   3 cups all-purpose flour
1/2 cup sugar
   3 teaspoons baking powder
1/2 teaspoon salt
1/2 cup cold butter
   1 egg
   1 cup buttermilk
   1 cup pitted dried plums, chopped
   1 tablespoon grated orange peel
TOPPING:
   1 egg
   1 tablespoon 2% milk
   2 tablespoons coarse sugar

**1.** In a large bowl, combine the flour, sugar, baking powder and salt. Cut in butter until mixture resembles coarse crumbs. Whisk egg and buttermilk; stir into crumb mixture just until moistened. Stir in plums and orange peel. Turn onto a floured surface; knead 10 times.

**2.** Divide the dough in half; pat each into a 7-in. circle. Cut each into six wedges. Separate wedges and place on a greased baking sheet. Combine egg and milk; brush over scones. Sprinkle with coarse sugar. Bake at 375° for 15-20 minutes or until golden brown. Serve warm. **Yield:** 1 dozen.

*Sugar Plum Scones*

# Butterscotch Pecan Bread

*Enjoy a slice of this moist, nutty bread with your morning cup of coffee...or bake several loaves to give as gifts. Everyone loves the crunchy pecans and old-fashioned butterscotch flavor.* —Angela Ochoa, Lake Elsinore, California

1/2 cup butter, softened
1/2 cup sugar
   3 eggs
   3 teaspoons vanilla extract
   2 cups all-purpose flour
   1 package (3.4 ounces) instant butterscotch pudding mix
   2 teaspoons baking powder
1/2 teaspoon salt
   1 cup milk
1-1/2 cups chopped pecans

**1.** In a large bowl, cream the butter and sugar until light and fluffy. Add eggs and vanilla; mix well. Combine the flour, pudding mix, baking powder and salt; add to creamed mixture alternately with milk. Fold in pecans.

**2.** Transfer to a greased 9-in. x 5-in. loaf pan. Bake at 350° for 55-65 minutes or until a toothpick inserted near the center comes out clean. Cool for 10 minutes before removing from pan to a wire rack. **Yield:** 1 loaf (16 slices).

# Gugelhopf

*You'll bring a taste of the Old World to your holiday table when you serve this time-honored German pastry. It's sure to please everyone...even those who don't care for fruitcake. If you like, substitute dried cherries or raisins for the other dried fruits.* —Karen Deaver, Babylon Village, New York

3-1/2 teaspoons active dry yeast
   1 cup warm 2% milk (110° to 115°)
   3 cups all-purpose flour
3/4 cup sugar
1/2 cup butter, softened
   4 teaspoons grated orange peel
Dash salt
   4 egg yolks
1/2 cup chopped dried apricots
1/2 cup dried cranberries
1/2 cup slivered almonds
Confectioners' sugar

**1.** In a small bowl, dissolve yeast in warm milk. Place the flour, sugar, butter, orange peel and salt in a food processor; cover and process until blended. Add egg yolks; cover and process just until moistened. While processing, gradually add milk mixture in a steady stream. Stir in the apricots, cranberries and almonds.

**2.** Transfer to a greased 9-in. decorative tube pan. Cover and let rise until doubled, about 1 hour. Bake at 375° for 30-35 minutes or until golden brown. Cool for 5 minutes before removing from pan to a wire rack to cool completely. Sprinkle with confectioners' sugar. **Yield:** 12 servings.

# Finnish Cinnamon Rolls

*These cinnamon-spiced goodies aren't too sweet, and the hint of cardamom offers a nice change of pace from traditional iced rolls. Prepare to hear raves!* —Mrs. Jim Albie, Brainerd, Minnesota

    1 package (1/4 ounce) active dry yeast
    1 teaspoon plus 1 cup sugar, *divided*
    1 cup warm water (110° to 115°)
    1 cup 2% milk (110° to 115°)
  1/2 cup butter, melted
    2 eggs
    8 to 12 cardamom seeds, crushed
    1 teaspoon salt
6-1/2 to 7 cups all-purpose flour
FILLING:
  1/2 cup sugar
1-1/2 teaspoons ground cinnamon
TOPPING:
    2 tablespoons brewed coffee
    2 teaspoons plus 2 tablespoons sugar, *divided*

**1.** In a large bowl, dissolve yeast and 1 teaspoon sugar in warm water. Add milk, butter, eggs, cardamom, salt, 3 cups flour and remaining sugar. Beat until smooth. Stir in enough remaining flour to form a soft dough (dough will be sticky).

**2.** Turn onto a floured surface; knead until smooth and elastic, about 6-8 minutes. Place in a greased bowl, turning once to grease the top. Cover and let rise in a warm place until doubled, about 1 hour.

**3.** In a small bowl, combine sugar and cinnamon. Punch dough down. Turn onto a lightly floured surface; divide in half. Roll one portion into an 18-in. x 10-in. rectangle; sprinkle with half of the sugar mixture to within 1/2 in. of edges.

**4.** Roll up jelly-roll style, starting with a long side; pinch seam to seal. Cut into 12 slices; place cut side down in a greased 13-in. x 9-in. baking dish. Repeat with remaining dough and sugar mixture.

**5.** Cover and let rise until nearly doubled, about 45 minutes. Bake at 350° for 18-22 minutes or until golden brown.

**6.** In a small bowl, combine coffee and 2 teaspoons sugar; brush over rolls. Sprinkle with remaining sugar. **Yield: 2 dozen.**

# Maple Bubble Bread

*This is my family's favorite breakfast bread. With a scrumptious topping of maple syrup and brown sugar, it's the perfect start to a special day.* —Hannah Cobb, Owings Mills, Maryland

    1 package (1/4 ounce) active dry yeast
  1/4 cup warm water (110° to 115°)
    1 cup warm 2% milk (110° to 115°)
  1/3 cup butter, melted
  1/4 cup sugar
    1 egg
    1 egg yolk
  1/2 teaspoon salt
    5 cups all-purpose flour

*Maple Bubble Bread*

TOPPING:
  2/3 cup maple syrup
    2 tablespoons butter
    1 cup packed brown sugar
  1/2 teaspoon ground cinnamon
    3 tablespoons butter, melted

**1.** In a large bowl, dissolve the yeast in warm water. Add the warm milk, butter, sugar, egg, egg yolk, salt and 3 cups flour. Beat on medium speed for 3 minutes. Stir in enough remaining flour to form a firm dough.

**2.** Turn onto a floured surface; knead until smooth and elastic, about 6-8 minutes. Place in a greased bowl, turning once to grease the top. Cover and let rise in a warm place until doubled, about 1 hour.

**3.** In a small saucepan, combine syrup and butter. Bring to a boil. Cook and stir for 3 minutes; set aside.

**4.** Punch dough down. Turn onto a lightly floured surface; divide into 20 pieces. Shape each into a roll. In a shallow bowl, combine brown sugar and cinnamon. Place melted butter in a separate shallow bowl. Dip buns in butter, then coat in brown sugar mixture.

**5.** Place eight rolls in a greased 10-in. fluted tube pan; drizzle with 1/3 cup syrup. Top with remaining rolls, syrup and brown sugar mixture. Cover and let rise until doubled, about 45 minutes.

**6.** Bake at 350° for 30-35 minutes or until golden brown. Cool for 10 minutes before inverting onto a serving plate. Serve warm. **Yield: 20 servings.**

*Pepperoni Cheese Twists (p. 42)*
*Cranberry-Mango Salsa with Tree Chips*

# Cranberry-Mango Salsa with Tree Chips

*This delightfully different salsa features a nice balance of sweet, tart and spicy. The accompanying tree-shaped chips are fun and easy to make using tortillas and a cookie cutter.*
—*Janice Christofferson, Eagle River, Wisconsin*

> 1 package (12 ounces) fresh *or* frozen cranberries
> 1 cup sugar
> 1 cup water
> 1 tablespoon cornstarch
> 1 tablespoon lime juice
> 1 medium mango, peeled and chopped
> 1 jalapeno pepper, seeded and chopped
> 1 green onion, chopped
> 1 tablespoon chopped red onion
> 1 tablespoon minced fresh cilantro
> 1/4 teaspoon ground cumin
> 10 spinach, tomato *and/or* plain tortillas (8 inches)

**1.** In a large saucepan, combine the cranberries, sugar and water. Cook over medium heat until the berries pop, about 15 minutes. Combine cornstarch and lime juice until smooth; add to cranberry mixture. Bring to a boil; cook and stir for 1-2 minutes or until thickened. Transfer to a large bowl; stir in the mango, jalapeno, onions, cilantro and cumin. Cool. Cover and refrigerate until serving.

**2.** Using a 3-inch tree-shaped cookie cutter, cut 10 tree shapes from each tortilla; place on ungreased baking sheets. Bake at 375° for 5-6 minutes or until crisp. Remove chips to wire racks to cool completely. Serve with salsa. **Yield:** 3-1/2 cups salsa (100 chips).

**Editor's Note:** When cutting hot peppers, disposable gloves are recommended. Avoid touching your face.

# Herbed Havarti in Pastry

*At holiday cocktail parties, I love surprising guests with this impressive Havarti baked inside puff pastry. The wrapped cheese is pleasantly seasoned with herbs and served alongside crackers and fresh fruit.* —*Darcy Truax, Coupeville, Washington*

> 1/2 cup dried parsley flakes
> 1 teaspoon dried thyme
> 1 teaspoon dried rosemary, crushed
> 1/2 teaspoon dried oregano
> 2 tablespoons Dijon mustard
> 2 blocks (8 ounces *each*) dill Havarti cheese
> 1 sheet frozen puff pastry, thawed
> 1 egg, beaten
> Coarse salt, optional
> Assorted crackers and fresh fruit

**1.** In a shallow bowl, combine the parsley, thyme, rosemary and oregano. Spread mustard over cheese blocks; roll in herbs to coat.

**2.** On a lightly floured surface, roll pastry to about 13 in. long (or long enough to fit cheese blocks end to end). Place cheese on pastry and fold pastry around cheese; trim excess dough. Pinch the edges to seal. Place seam side down on an ungreased baking sheet.

**3.** Brush pastry with egg. With floured cutters, cut decorative shapes from dough scraps if desired; arrange over the top and brush with egg. Sprinkle with salt if desired. Bake at 375° for 20-25 minutes or until puffed and golden brown. Serve warm with crackers and fruit. **Yield:** 16 servings.

*Herbed Havarti in Pastry*

# Pepperoni Cheese Twists

*Refrigerated dough keeps these snacks fuss-free. They're great all by themselves…or try them with a simple antipasto of peppers, olives and cheeses.* —Josephine Piro, Easton, Pennsylvania

    3 tablespoons finely chopped oil-packed sun-dried
       tomatoes plus 1 teaspoon oil from the jar
    1/3 cup finely chopped pepperoni
    1/3 cup shredded Parmesan cheese
1-1/2 teaspoons minced fresh rosemary *or* 1/2 teaspoon
       dried rosemary, crushed
    1 teaspoon water
Dash garlic powder
Dash pepper
    1 tube (13.8 ounces) refrigerated pizza crust

**1.** In a small bowl, combine the tomatoes and their oil, pepperoni, cheese, rosemary, water, garlic powder and pepper.

**2.** On a lightly floured surface, roll dough into a 14-in. x 10-in. rectangle. Spread tomato mixture lengthwise over half of dough. Fold dough over filling: press edges to seal. Cut widthwise into fourteen 1-in.-wide strips. Fold each strip in half; twist two or three times. Place 1 in. apart on a greased baking sheet.

**3.** Bake at 425° for 6-8 minutes or until twists are golden brown. **Yield:** 14 cheese twists.

# Pesto-Pepper Cheese Spread

*I get tons of recipe requests whenever I bring this zippy spread to a party. Use convenient store-bought pesto or your favorite homemade version.* —Lara Pennell, Mauldin, South Carolina

*Pesto-Pepper Cheese Spread*

    2 packages (8 ounces *each*) cream cheese, softened
    2 cups crumbled goat cheese
    2 tablespoons olive oil
    1 teaspoon dried thyme
    2 garlic cloves, minced
    3 tablespoons prepared pesto
    1/3 cup chopped roasted sweet red peppers
Assorted crackers *or* sliced French bread baguette

**1.** In a large bowl, combine the cream cheese, goat cheese, oil, thyme and garlic.

**2.** Line a 1-qt. bowl with plastic wrap. Place a third of the cheese mixture in bowl; top with pesto, half of the remaining cheese mixture, the peppers and remaining cheese mixture. Cover and refrigerate for at least 3 hours.

**3.** Invert cheese mixture onto a serving plate; discard plastic wrap. Serve with crackers. **Yield:** 3 cups.

# Cranberry Spritzers

*Refreshing and slightly tart, this ruby-red beverage from our Test Kitchen is the perfect thirst-quencher for Christmas gatherings. Give it a special look in wine glasses with a lemon-twist garnish.*

    4 cups cranberry juice, chilled
    1 cup ruby red grapefruit juice, chilled
    1/2 cup sugar
    1/4 cup lemon juice
    1 bottle (1 liter) club soda, chilled
GARNISH:
Lemon twists

In a pitcher, combine cranberry juice, grapefruit juice, sugar and lemon juice; chill until serving. Just before serving, stir in club soda. Serve in wine glasses. Garnish as desired. **Yield:** 8 servings (2 quarts).

# Cheese-Olive Cream Puffs

*These savory bites always bake up golden brown and delicious. The tasty cheese-and-olive filling goes inside the cooled puffs just before serving.* —Arline Hofland, Deer Lodge, Montana

    1 cup water
    1/2 cup butter, cubed
    1/2 teaspoon salt
    1 cup all-purpose flour
    4 eggs
FILLING:
    2 packages (8 ounces *each*) cream cheese, softened
    1 cup (8 ounces) sour cream
    1 teaspoon lemon-pepper seasoning
    2 cups (8 ounces) crumbled blue cheese
    1 cup chopped pimiento-stuffed olives

**1.** In a large saucepan, bring the water, butter and salt to a boil. Add flour all at once and stir until a smooth ball forms. Remove from the heat; let stand for 5 minutes. Add eggs, one at a time, beating well after each addition. Continue beating until mixture is smooth and shiny.

**2.** Drop by rounded teaspoonfuls 3 in. apart onto parchment paper-lined baking sheets. Bake at 400° for 25-30 minutes or until golden brown.

**3.** Remove to wire racks. Immediately split puffs open; remove tops and set aside. Discard soft dough from inside. Cool puffs.

**4.** For filling, in a small bowl, beat cream cheese until fluffy. Beat in sour cream and lemon-pepper. Fold in blue cheese and olives. Fill the cream puffs just before serving. **Yield:** 3 dozen.

## Crab Artichoke Dip With Toasted Pitas

*The first year I was married, I brought this appetizer to our family's Christmas Eve celebration. The dip and toasted pitas went over so well, I've been bringing them ever since.*
—Tabetha Carson, Independence, Missouri

    1 small onion, chopped
    1 tablespoon butter
    2 cups mayonnaise
    1 can (14 ounces) water-packed artichoke hearts, rinsed, drained and coarsely chopped
    1 cup grated Parmesan cheese
    1 cup (4 ounces) shredded part-skim mozzarella cheese
4-1/2 teaspoons lemon juice
    4 teaspoons Worcestershire sauce
    1/2 teaspoon celery salt
    4 cans (6 ounces *each*) lump crabmeat, drained
PITAS:
    6 whole gyro-style pitas (6 inches)
    1/3 cup olive oil

**1.** In a small skillet, saute onion in butter until tender. Transfer to a large bowl; add the mayonnaise, artichokes, cheeses, lemon juice, Worcestershire sauce and celery salt. Gently stir in crab. Transfer to a greased 2-qt. baking dish. Bake at 350° for 25-30 minutes or until bubbly.

**2.** Cut each pita bread into eight wedges. Separate each wedge into two triangles. Place the triangles rough side up on baking sheet; brush with olive oil. Broil 4-6 in. from the heat for 1-2 minutes or until golden brown. Serve with warm dip. **Yield:** 6 cups dip (8 dozen chips).

## Around the World Tapenade

*Featuring flavors from around the globe, this recipe is a trip for the taste buds! Chopping the ingredients in a food processor keeps things quick and easy.* —Kim Rila, Leesburg, Virginia

    1/2 cup chopped roasted sweet red pepper
    1/2 cup pitted Greek olives
    1/4 cup chopped poblano pepper
    2 tablespoons lemon juice
    2 tablespoons olive oil
    1 tablespoon minced fresh parsley
    1 tablespoon capers, drained

Around the World Tapenade

    2 garlic cloves, minced
    1/4 teaspoon dried thyme
    16 slices French bread baguette (1/2 inch thick), toasted

In a food processor, combine the first nine ingredients; cover and process until blended. Spoon 1 tablespoon tapenade onto each baguette slice. **Yield:** 16 appetizers.

**Editor's Note:** When cutting hot peppers, disposable gloves are recommended. Avoid touching your face.

## Smoked Salmon Dip In Pumpernickel

*I got this recipe from my brother, who is a fabulous cook, and it has become a staple at Christmastime. The smoky salmon blends wonderfully with the cream cheese. Adjust the amount of hot sauce to suit your taste.* —Kathy Smuz, Clearwater, Florida

    1 round loaf (1 pound) pumpernickel bread
    1/2 pound smoked salmon fillet
    1 package (8 ounces) cream cheese, softened
    1/2 cup 2% milk
    3 green onions, chopped
    2 tablespoons lemon juice
    2 teaspoons Worcestershire sauce
    1/2 teaspoon hot pepper sauce
    1/4 cup capers, drained
Assorted fresh vegetables

**1.** Cut top fourth off of the loaf of bread; carefully hollow out bottom, leaving a 1/2-in. shell. Cube removed bread; set aside.

**2.** In a food processor, combine the salmon, cream cheese, milk, onions, lemon juice, Worcestershire sauce and pepper sauce; cover and process until smooth. Stir in capers.

**3.** Fill bread shell with salmon dip. Serve with vegetables and reserved bread cubes. **Yield:** 2-1/2 cups.

*Fruit-Stuffed Crown Roast*

# Fruit-Stuffed Crown Roast

*Absolutely sensational is the only way to describe this crown roast! Moist and full of fruit-flavored stuffing, it's a natural choice for any dinner that calls for a special presentation.*
—*Shaaron Hetland, Chilliwack, British Columbia*

1-1/2 cups red currant jelly
1/2 cup orange liqueur *or* juice
1 pork crown rib roast (16 ribs and about 8 pounds)
1/4 cup butter, cubed
1 large onion, chopped
1 celery rib, chopped
6 cups unseasoned stuffing cubes
1 can (15-1/4 ounces) apricot halves, drained and quartered
1 can (8 ounces) sliced water chestnuts, drained
1 large tart apple, peeled and chopped
1 egg, beaten
1 teaspoon salt
1/2 teaspoon rubbed sage
1/2 teaspoon dried thyme

**1.** In a small saucepan, heat jelly and orange liqueur over low heat until jelly is melted; brush over roast. Place roast on a rack in a large shallow roasting pan. Cover rib ends with foil. Bake, uncovered, at 350° for 2 hours.

**2.** In a large skillet, melt butter over medium heat. Add onion and celery; cook and stir until tender. Transfer to a large bowl; add the remaining ingredients and mix well.

**3.** Carefully spoon stuffing into center of roast. Bake 1 hour longer or until a meat thermometer reads 160° in the meat and stuffing.

**4.** Transfer to a serving platter; let stand for 10-15 minutes. Discard foil. Cut between ribs to serve. **Yield:** 16 servings.

**Editor's Note:** Extra stuffing may be baked, covered, in a greased baking dish for 45-60 minutes or until a thermometer reads 160°.

# Brunswick Stew

*Everyone will warm up to this hearty stew after a long day of sledding, skiing or other fun activities in the frosty outdoors. Use leftover or rotisserie chicken to keep the preparation easy.*
—*Patty Stremsterfer, Pleasant Plains, Illinois*

1/4 cup butter, cubed
2 medium onions, chopped
6 cups chicken broth, *divided*
5 cups cubed cooked chicken
1 package (16 ounces) frozen corn, thawed
1 package (16 ounces) frozen lima beans, thawed
4 medium potatoes, peeled and diced
3 cans (14-1/2 ounces *each*) diced tomatoes, undrained
2 celery ribs, chopped
1 cup water
1/4 teaspoon *each* dried basil, marjoram and thyme
1/4 teaspoon hot pepper sauce
1 tablespoon cornstarch

**1.** In a stockpot, melt butter. Add onions; saute until tender. Stir in 5 cups chicken broth, chicken, corn, beans, potatoes, tomatoes, celery, water, herbs and pepper sauce. Bring to a boil. Reduce heat; cover and simmer for 45 minutes.

**2.** Combine the cornstarch and remaining chicken broth until smooth; gradually stir into the stew. Bring to a boil; cook and stir for 2 minutes or until slightly thickened. **Yield:** 14 servings (1-1/2 cups each).

*Brunswick Stew*

# Spinach Lasagna Roll-Ups

*With five kinds of cheese, these pasta roll-ups are so flavorful. Keep them in mind when you want an impressive main course for special guests.* —Mary Jane Jones, Williamston, West Virginia

    10 uncooked lasagna noodles
     1 package (8 ounces) cream cheese, softened
     2 packages (10 ounces *each*) frozen chopped spinach, thawed and squeezed dry
     1 carton (15 ounces) ricotta cheese
     2 cups (8 ounces) shredded part-skim mozzarella cheese
     1 cup grated Parmesan cheese
1-1/2 teaspoons Italian seasoning
   1/4 teaspoon salt
SAUCE:
     3 tablespoons butter
     4 tablespoons all-purpose flour
   1/2 teaspoon pepper
   1/4 teaspoon salt
     2 cups chicken broth
     1 cup heavy whipping cream
TOPPING:
   1/2 cup shredded Gruyere cheese
   1/2 cup grated Parmesan cheese

**1.** Cook lasagna noodles according to package directions; drain. In a large bowl, beat cream cheese until smooth. Stir in the spinach, ricotta, mozzarella, Parmesan, Italian seasoning and salt. Spread 1/2 cup cheese mixture over each noodle; carefully roll up.

**2.** For sauce, in a large saucepan, melt butter over medium heat. Whisk in the flour, pepper and salt until smooth. Gradu-ally whisk in broth. Bring to a boil; cook and stir for 2 minutes or until thickened. Remove from the heat; stir in cream.

**3.** Pour 1 cup sauce into a greased 13-in. x 9-in. baking dish. Cut lasagna roll-ups in half widthwise; place cut side down in dish. Top with remaining sauce; sprinkle with Gruyere and Parmesan.

**4.** Cover and bake at 350° for 20-25 minutes. Uncover; bake 10 minutes longer or until bubbly. Let stand for 15 minutes before serving. **Yield:** 10 servings.

# Cherry Mincemeat Mold

*This gelatin has a touch of sweetness from dark cherries and a nice crunch from apples and nuts. Its red color makes it festive for December meals.* —Nella Parker, Hersey, Michigan

     1 can (15 ounces) pitted dark sweet cherries
     2 packages (3 ounces *each*) cherry gelatin
     2 cups boiling water
     2 tablespoons lemon juice
   1/2 cup chopped tart apple
   1/2 cup prepared mincemeat
   1/2 cup chopped walnuts

**1.** Drain cherries, reserving juice in a 2-cup measuring cup; add enough water to measure 1-1/2 cups. Cut cherries in half; set aside.

**2.** In a large bowl, dissolve gelatin in boiling water. Stir in the lemon juice and cherry juice mixture. Refrigerate until partially set. Fold in the apple, mincemeat, walnuts and cherries. Transfer to a 6-cup ring mold coated with cooking spray. Refrigerate until firm. Unmold onto a serving plate. **Yield:** 8 servings.

# Herbed Seafood Casserole

*A friend shared this recipe when I needed a seafood dish for my annual Christmas Eve buffet. The casserole is wonderfully rich and creamy.* —Donna Schmuland, Wetaskiwin, Alberta

1-1/2 cups uncooked long grain rice
     2 tablespoons minced fresh parsley
1-1/2 teaspoons snipped fresh dill *or* 1/2 teaspoon dill weed
     3 celery ribs, thinly sliced
     1 medium onion, finely chopped
     1 medium carrot, shredded
     2 tablespoons butter
     3 garlic cloves, minced
   1/2 teaspoon salt
   1/4 teaspoon pepper
SEAFOOD:
     1 pound uncooked medium shrimp, peeled and deveined
     1 pound bay scallops
     1 can (16 ounces) crabmeat, drained, flaked and cartilage removed
     5 tablespoons butter, cubed
   1/4 cup all-purpose flour

*Spinach Lasagna Roll-Ups*

1-1/2 cups half-and-half cream
   1 package (8 ounces) cream cheese, cubed
1-1/2 teaspoons snipped fresh dill *or* 1/2 teaspoon dill
     weed
  1/2 teaspoon salt
  1/4 teaspoon pepper
  1/4 teaspoon dried thyme
TOPPING:
1-1/2 cups soft bread crumbs
   2 tablespoons butter, melted

**1.** Cook rice according to package directions; stir in parsley and dill. In a large skillet, saute the celery, onion and carrot in butter until crisp-tender. Add the garlic, salt and pepper; cook 1 minute longer. Stir into rice mixture; set aside.

**2.** Fill a large saucepan two-thirds full with water. Bring to a boil. Reduce heat; carefully add shrimp. Cook, uncovered, for 30 seconds. Add scallops; cook 2-3 minutes longer or until shrimp turn pink and scallops are firm and opaque. Drain, reserving 1 cup cooking liquid. Place seafood in a large bowl; stir in crab and set aside.

**3.** In another saucepan, melt butter; stir in flour until smooth. Gradually stir in cream and reserved cooking liquid. Bring to a boil; cook and stir for 2 minutes or until thickened and bubbly. Reduce heat; stir in cream cheese and seasonings until cheese is melted. Pour over seafood mixture and stir until blended.

**4.** Place rice mixture in a greased 13-in. x 9-in. baking dish; top with seafood mixture. Combine bread crumbs and butter; sprinkle over the top. Bake, uncovered, at 325° for 50-55 minutes or until golden brown. **Yield:** 12 servings.

# Lemon Pudding Dessert

*A piece of this fluffy dessert is pure heaven! We indulge in this yummy treat during the holidays, and I love it because you can make it in advance and keep it in the fridge until serving time.*
       —Janice Hurd, Church Hill, Tennessee

   1 cup all-purpose flour
  1/2 cup chopped pecans
  1/2 cup butter, melted
   1 tablespoon sugar
FILLING:
   1 package (8 ounces) cream cheese, softened
   1 cup confectioners' sugar
   1 carton (12 ounces) frozen whipped topping,
     thawed, *divided*
   4 cups cold 2% milk
   3 packages (3.4 ounces *each*) instant lemon pudding
     mix

**1.** In a small bowl, combine the flour, pecans, butter and sugar. Press onto the bottom of a greased 13-in. x 9-in. baking dish. Bake at 350° for 12-15 minutes or until edges are lightly browned. Cool completely on a wire rack.

**2.** In a large bowl, beat cream cheese and confectioners' sugar until smooth. Fold in half of the whipped topping. Spread over crust.

*Lemon Pudding Dessert*

**3.** In a large bowl, whisk milk and pudding mixes for 2 minutes. Let stand for 2 minutes or until soft-set. Spread over cream cheese layer; top with remaining whipped topping. Refrigerate until chilled. **Yield:** 20 servings.

# Bacon-Cheddar French Bread

*This tasty loaf features a soft, tender texture with lots of flavor from cheese and Italian herbs. It's great alongside a fresh green salad and pasta.*    —Loraine Meyer, Bend, Oregon

   2 packages (1/4 ounce *each*) active dry yeast
   2 cups warm water (110° to 115°)
   2 cups (8 ounces) shredded sharp cheddar cheese
   6 bacon strips, cooked and crumbled
  1/4 cup sour cream
   1 tablespoon butter, melted
   2 teaspoons salt
   1 teaspoon Italian seasoning
   6 to 6-1/2 cups all-purpose flour

**1.** In a large bowl, dissolve yeast in warm water. Add the cheese, bacon, sour cream, butter, salt, Italian seasoning and 4 cups flour. Beat until smooth. Stir in enough remaining flour to form a soft dough (dough will be sticky).

**2.** Turn onto a floured surface; knead until smooth and elastic, about 6-8 minutes. Place in a greased bowl, turning once to grease the top. Cover and let rise in a warm place until doubled, about 1 hour.

**3.** Punch dough down. Turn onto a lightly floured surface; divide in half. Shape into 15-in.-long loaves. Place on two greased baking sheets. Cover and let rise in a warm place until doubled, about 30 minutes.

**4.** With a sharp knife, make five shallow slashes across the top of each loaf. Bake at 425° for 15-20 minutes or until golden brown. Remove from the pans to wire racks to cool. **Yield:** 2 loaves (16 slices each).

*Antipasto Spinach Salad*

## Antipasto Spinach Salad

*A jazzed-up Italian dressing tops off this fresh-tasting medley. With lots of red and green color, this is a festive starter for your Christmas feast.* —Roxanne Chan, Albany, California

    1/3 cup Italian salad dressing
       1 tablespoon dried currants
       1 tablespoon capers, drained
    1/2 teaspoon lemon-pepper seasoning
    1/2 teaspoon grated lemon peel
       6 cups fresh baby spinach
       2 cups torn radicchio leaves
       1 can (15 ounces) white kidney *or* cannellini beans,
          rinsed and drained
       1 jar (7-1/2 ounces) marinated quartered artichoke
          hearts, drained
       1 small red onion, thinly sliced
    1/4 pound hard salami, finely chopped
    1/2 cup cubed part-skim mozzarella cheese
    1/2 cup julienned roasted sweet red pepper
    1/4 cup minced fresh parsley
       2 tablespoons shredded Parmesan cheese

**1.** In a small microwave-safe bowl, combine the first five ingredients. Microwave, uncovered, on high for 30-45 seconds or until heated through.

**2.** In a salad bowl, combine the spinach, radicchio, beans, artichokes, onion, salami, mozzarella, pepper and parsley. Drizzle with dressing; toss to coat. Sprinkle with Parmesan cheese. Serve immediately. **Yield:** 10 servings.

## Tip Roast & Onion Cream Sauce

*I combined two favorite recipes to come up with this tender beef tip roast. The accompanying onion-cream gravy is delicious over the meat.* —Phyllis Waterman, Rockford, Illinois

    1/3 cup red wine vinegar
    1/4 cup ketchup
       2 tablespoons canola oil
       2 tablespoons soy sauce
       2 tablespoons Worcestershire sauce
       1 teaspoon salt
       1 teaspoon prepared mustard
    1/4 teaspoon garlic powder
    1/4 teaspoon pepper
       1 beef sirloin tip roast (4 pounds)
SAUCE:
       2 tablespoons butter
       1 tablespoon all-purpose flour
       1 cup milk
       1 cup heavy whipping cream
       1 envelope onion mushroom soup mix

**1.** In a large resealable plastic bag, combine the first nine ingredients for marinade. Add the beef; seal bag and turn to coat. Refrigerate for 8 hours or overnight. Drain and discard marinade.

**2.** Place the roast on a rack in a shallow roasting pan. Bake, uncovered, at 350° for 1-3/4 to 2-1/2 hours or until meat reaches desired doneness (for medium-rare, a meat thermometer should read 145°; medium, 160°; well-done, 170°). Transfer roast to a serving platter. Let stand for 10 minutes before slicing.

**3.** For sauce, melt the butter in a small saucepan; stir in the flour until smooth. Gradually add the milk, heavy whipping cream and onion mushroom soup mix. Bring to a boil. Cook and stir for 2 minutes or until thickened. Serve with roast. **Yield:** 8 servings (2 cups sauce).

## Roasted Potatoes, Carrots & Leeks

*Simply seasoned and flavored with garlic, this fantastic side dish will complement just about any entree. The colorful veggies are easy to prepare and look attractive on a holiday buffet...but you'll want to keep this recipe in mind for meals all year long.* —Janice Mitchell, Aurora, Colorado

       2 pounds small red potatoes
       1 pound fresh baby carrots
       3 tablespoons butter, melted
       1 tablespoon olive oil
       1 teaspoon salt
    1/4 teaspoon pepper
       6 medium leeks (white portions only), halved
          lengthwise, cleaned and cut into 1-inch lengths
       2 garlic cloves, minced

**1.** Scrub and quarter potatoes; place in a large bowl. Add the carrots, butter, oil, salt and pepper; toss to coat. Arrange in a single layer in two ungreased 15-in. x 10-in. x 1-in. baking pans.

**2.** Bake at 425° for 25 minutes. Add leeks and garlic; bake 20-25 minutes longer or until tender, stirring occasionally. **Yield:** 12 servings (3/4 cup each).

*Chocolate Truffle Raspberry Cheesecake (p. 50)*
*Roasted Potatoes, Carrots & Leeks*
*Tip Roast & Onion Cream Sauce*

# Shoepeg Corn Supreme

*Dress up canned corn with green pepper, cream of celery soup and cheddar cheese for a deluxe side dish. With a butter-flavored cracker coating, this comfort food is sure to disappear in a hurry.*
—*Linda Roberson, Collierville, Tennessee*

    1 small green pepper, chopped
    1 small onion, chopped
    1 celery rib, chopped
    2 tablespoons olive oil
    2 cans (11 ounces *each*) shoepeg *or* white corn, drained
    1 can (10-3/4 ounces) condensed cream of celery soup, undiluted
    1 cup (8 ounces) sour cream
    1/2 cup shredded sharp cheddar cheese
    1/4 teaspoon pepper
1-1/2 cups crushed butter-flavored crackers
    3 tablespoons butter, melted

**1.** In a large skillet, saute the green pepper, onion and celery in oil until tender. Remove from the heat; stir in the corn, soup, sour cream, cheese and pepper. Transfer to a greased 11-in. x 7-in. baking dish.

**2.** Combine cracker crumbs and butter; sprinkle over the top. Bake, uncovered, at 350° for 25-30 minutes or until bubbly. **Yield:** 8 servings.

*Shoepeg Corn Supreme*

# Chocolate Truffle Raspberry Cheesecake

(Pictured on page 49)

*No matter how full they are, guests won't be able to pass up this showstopper of a dessert that stars a velvety truffle layer atop raspberry-swirled cheesecake. It's absolutely divine!*
—*Heidi Vawdrey, Riverton, Utah*

    2 cups cream-filled chocolate sandwich cookie crumbs
    2 tablespoons butter, melted
**FILLING:**
    2 packages (8 ounces *each*) cream cheese, softened
    3/4 cup sugar
    1 cup white baking chips, melted and cooled
    1/3 cup heavy whipping cream
    3 teaspoons vanilla extract
    3 eggs, lightly beaten
    3 tablespoons seedless raspberry jam
**TRUFFLE LAYER:**
1-1/4 cups heavy whipping cream
    1/3 cup sugar
    2 cups (12 ounces) semisweet chocolate chips
    3 tablespoons seedless raspberry jam
Fresh raspberries and mint leaves, optional

**1.** In a large bowl, combine cookie crumbs and butter. Press onto the bottom and 1 in. up the sides of a greased 9-in. springform pan; set aside.

**2.** In a large bowl, beat cream cheese and sugar until smooth. Beat in the melted chips, cream and vanilla. Add eggs; beat on low speed just until combined. Pour into crust. Drop jam by teaspoonfuls onto filling; swirl with a knife. Place pan on a baking sheet.

**3.** Bake at 325° for 45-50 minutes or until the center is almost set. Cool on a wire rack for 10 minutes. Carefully run a knife around edge of pan to loosen; cool 1 hour longer.

**4.** For truffle layer, in a small heavy saucepan, combine cream and sugar. Bring to a boil over medium heat, stirring constantly. Remove from the heat; stir in chips and jam until smooth. Transfer to a bowl; refrigerate for about 1 hour or until slightly set. Beat for 1-2 minutes or until light and fluffy. Gently spread over cheesecake. Refrigerate overnight.

**5.** Garnish cheesecake with raspberries and mint if desired. **Yield:** 16 servings.

# Sweet and Spicy Tossed Salad

*Here's a tongue-tingling medley that combines sweet cherries and walnuts spiced with ginger, cayenne and curry. Plus, the maple vinaigrette is delightfully different from other salad dressings. If you like, toss in some dried cranberries or raisins.*
—*Mardee Thomas, Fortson, Georgia*

1-1/3 cups walnut halves
    2 tablespoons butter, melted
    3 tablespoons sugar

1/4 teaspoon ground ginger
1/8 teaspoon curry powder
1/8 teaspoon salt
1/8 teaspoon cayenne pepper
DRESSING:
1/3 cup cider vinegar
3 tablespoons maple syrup
1 tablespoon Dijon mustard
1/4 teaspoon salt
1/4 teaspoon pepper
2/3 cup olive oil
SALAD:
2 packages (5 ounces *each*) spring mix salad greens
1 package (5 ounces) dried cherries
1 small red onion, thinly sliced
1 cup shaved Parmesan cheese

1. In a small bowl, combine the walnuts and butter. Add the sugar, ginger, curry, salt and cayenne; toss to coat. Spread in a single layer in an ungreased 15-in. x 10-in. x 1-in. baking pan. Bake at 350° for 8-10 minutes or until golden brown, stirring occasionally. Set aside.

2. In a small bowl, whisk the vinegar, syrup, mustard, salt and pepper. Gradually whisk in oil. In a salad bowl, combine the salad greens, cherries and onion. Drizzle with dressing and toss to coat. Sprinkle with cheese and toasted walnuts. Serve immediately. **Yield:** 22 servings (3/4 cup each).

## Steakhouse Mushroom Casserole

*This meatless casserole is one of my all-time favorites. Loaded with mushrooms and draped in a rich sauce, it's a home-style side dish that will have everyone scooping up seconds.*
—Rosemary Janz, Concord, North Carolina

2 pounds sliced fresh mushrooms
3/4 cup butter, *divided*
1 cup heavy whipping cream
1 egg yolk
1 tablespoon minced fresh parsley
1 tablespoon lemon juice
1 teaspoon salt
1/2 teaspoon paprika
2 cups crushed butter-flavored crackers

1. In a large skillet, saute mushrooms in batches in 1/4 cup butter until mushrooms are tender and liquid is evaporated. In a large bowl, whisk the heavy whipping cream, egg yolk, parsley, lemon juice, salt and paprika. Add mushrooms and stir until blended.

2. Transfer to a greased 8-inch square baking dish. Melt remaining butter; stir in cracker crumbs until blended. Sprinkle over mushroom mixture. Cover and refrigerate overnight.

3. Remove from the refrigerator 30 minutes before baking. Bake, uncovered, at 350° for 30-35 minutes or until a thermometer reads 160° and the topping is golden brown. **Yield:** 8 servings.

*Big-Batch Yeast Rolls*

## Big-Batch Yeast Rolls

*The egg wash on these golden-brown rolls gives them a pretty look for holiday entertaining. Light and tender, they have just a hint of sweetness.* —Anna Meyer, Fort Branch, Indiana

2 packages (1/4 ounce *each*) active dry yeast
1/2 cup warm water (110° to 115°)
2-1/2 cups warm 2% milk (110° to 115°)
1/2 cup butter, melted
1/2 cup mashed potato flakes
1 cup sugar
3 eggs
2-1/2 teaspoons salt
7 to 7-1/2 cups all-purpose flour
1 tablespoon cold water

1. In a large bowl, dissolve yeast in warm water. In another bowl, combine milk and butter; stir in potato flakes. Let stand for 1 minute. Add the milk mixture, sugar, 2 eggs, salt and 3 cups flour to yeast mixture; beat until smooth. Add enough remaining flour to form a soft dough.

2. Turn onto a floured surface; knead until smooth and elastic, about 6-8 minutes. Place in a greased bowl, turning once to grease the top. Cover and let rise in a warm place until doubled, about 1 hour.

3. Punch the dough down; divide into 36 pieces. Shape each into a ball. Place 2 in. apart on greased baking sheets. Cover and let rise until doubled, about 30 minutes. Beat remaining egg and cold water; brush over rolls. Bake at 350° for 12-15 minutes or until golden brown. **Yield:** 3 dozen.

*Pear Gingerbread Cake Roll*

*Christmas just wouldn't be complete without a home-baked pie, frosted layer cake or other special delight—the kind you dream about all year long!*

# Pear Gingerbread Cake Roll

*Crave the taste of gingerbread at Christmastime? Why stop at making cutout cookies? Enjoy this elegant swirled dessert. It dresses up a spiced molasses cake with a luscious pear filling.*
—Gwen Beauchamp, Lancaster, Texas

    3 eggs
    3 egg yolks
2/3 cup sugar
    2 tablespoons butter, melted
    2 tablespoons molasses
3/4 cup cake flour
    1 teaspoon baking powder
    1 teaspoon *each* ground ginger, cinnamon and
        allspice
    2 to 3 teaspoons confectioners' sugar
**FILLING:**
    2 medium pears, peeled and finely chopped
    1 tablespoon butter
    2 tablespoons pear brandy *or* brandy
    1 cup heavy whipping cream
    2 tablespoons confectioners' sugar
1/2 teaspoon ground cinnamon
1/4 teaspoon ground ginger
Additional confectioners' sugar and ground cinnamon,
    optional

**1.** Line a 15-in. x 10-in. x 1-in. baking pan with waxed paper; grease and flour the pan and paper. Set aside. In a large bowl, beat eggs and egg yolks for 3 minutes. Gradually add sugar; beat for 2 minutes or until mixture becomes thick and lemon-colored. Beat in butter and molasses. Combine the flour, baking powder and spices; fold into egg mixture. Spread batter into prepared pan.

**2.** Bake at 375° for 9-11 minutes or until cake springs back when lightly touched. Cool in pan for 5 minutes. Turn cake onto a kitchen towel dusted with confectioners' sugar. Gently peel off waxed paper. Roll up cake in towel jelly-roll style, starting with a short side. Cool completely on a wire rack.

**3.** For filling, in a small skillet, saute pears in butter until tender. Remove from the heat; stir in brandy. Cool completely. In a large bowl, beat the cream, confectioners' sugar, cinnamon and ginger until stiff peaks form. Gently fold in the pear mixture.

**4.** Unroll cake and spread filling over cake to within 1/2 in. of edges. Roll up again. Cover and refrigerate for 1 hour before serving. Dust with additional confectioners' sugar and cinnamon if desired. **Yield:** 10 servings.

# Spiced Fruit Crisp

*When it comes to a heartwarming treat on a chilly winter's day, this home-style crisp is hard to beat. The gingersnap-crumb topping nicely accents the apples, pears, raisins and dates.*
—Pat Habiger, Spearville, Kansas

3-1/2 cups chopped peeled tart apples
3-1/2 cups chopped peeled fresh pears
    1/4 cup chopped dates
    1/4 cup golden raisins
    1/4 cup molasses
    3/4 teaspoon ground cinnamon
    1/2 teaspoon ground ginger
    1/8 teaspoon ground nutmeg
    1/8 teaspoon ground cloves
**TOPPING:**
    9 gingersnap cookies, crushed
    1/4 cup sugar
    1/4 cup packed brown sugar
    2 tablespoons all-purpose flour
    1/4 cup cold butter
Whipped cream, optional

**1.** In a large bowl, combine the first nine ingredients. Transfer to a greased 11-in. x 7-in. baking dish.

**2.** In a small bowl, combine the cookie crumbs, sugar, brown sugar and flour. Cut in butter until mixture resembles coarse crumbs. Sprinkle over fruit mixture. Bake at 375° for 40-45 minutes or until topping is golden brown and fruit is tender. Serve with whipped cream if desired. **Yield:** 8 servings.

*Spiced Fruit Crisp*

# Grasshopper Pie

*My family looks forward to this fluffy pie every Christmas. No one can resist the combination of refreshing mint and luscious chocolate. Plus, the six-ingredient recipe is a snap to prepare— and the pretty pastel green color is festive for the occasion.*
*—Lindsey Dorn, New Glarus, Wisconsin*

1-1/2 cups plus 1 tablespoon chocolate wafer crumbs, *divided*
   5 tablespoons butter, melted
  24 large marshmallows
2/3 cup plus 1 cup heavy whipping cream, *divided*
   2 tablespoons clear creme de cacao
   2 tablespoons green creme de menthe

**1.** Combine 1-1/2 cups wafer crumbs and butter. Press into an ungreased 9-in. pie plate. Bake at 350° for 5-7 minutes or until set. Cool on a wire rack.

**2.** In a large heavy saucepan, combine the marshmallows and 2/3 cup heavy whipping cream; cook and stir over low heat until marshmallows are melted.

**3.** Remove from the heat. Stir in the creme de cacao and creme de menthe. Transfer to a small bowl; refrigerate for 1 hour or until slightly thickened.

**4.** In a large bowl, beat the remaining heavy whipping cream until stiff peaks form; fold into the marshmallow mixture. Pour into the prepared crust. Sprinkle with the remaining wafer crumbs. Refrigerate for several hours or overnight. **Yield:** 8 servings.

*Grasshopper Pie*

# German Apple Cake

*Tender apple slices and a simple confectioners'-sugar drizzle make this old-world treat yummy and comforting. It's especially good served warm with a scoop of vanilla ice cream.*
*—Tracey Rosato, Markham, Ontario*

 1/2 cup butter, softened
 2/3 cup sugar
   2 eggs
   4 teaspoons milk
 1/8 teaspoon lemon extract
   2 cups all-purpose flour
2-1/2 teaspoons baking powder
 1/8 teaspoon salt
   2 medium tart apples, peeled and thinly sliced
**DRIZZLE:**
   1 cup confectioners' sugar
   2 tablespoons butter, softened
   2 to 3 teaspoons milk

**1.** In a large bowl, cream butter and sugar until light and fluffy. Add eggs; mix well. Beat in milk and extract. Combine the flour, baking powder and salt; beat into creamed mixture just until moistened. With lightly floured hands, pat into a greased 9-in. springform pan. Arrange apples over the top.

**2.** Bake at 350° for 40-50 minutes or until a toothpick inserted near the center comes out clean. Cool on a wire rack for 10 minutes before removing from pan. Combine the confectioners' sugar, butter and milk; drizzle over the top. **Yield:** 10 servings.

# Devil's Food Cake with Chocolate Fudge Frosting

*This recipe received several blue ribbons at our state fair. The made-from-scratch chocolate layer cake topped with a fudgy homemade frosting is truly a can't-miss dessert.*
*—Donna Carman, Tulsa, Oklahoma*

   3 ounces unsweetened chocolate, chopped
 1/2 cup butter, softened
2-1/4 cups packed brown sugar
   3 eggs
1-1/2 teaspoons vanilla extract
2-1/4 cups cake flour
   1 teaspoon baking soda
 1/2 teaspoon salt
 1/2 teaspoon baking powder
   1 cup water
   1 cup (8 ounces) sour cream
**FROSTING:**
 1/2 cup butter, cubed
   4 ounces unsweetened chocolate, chopped
3-3/4 cups confectioners' sugar
 1/2 cup milk
   2 teaspoons vanilla extract

**1.** In a microwave, melt chocolate; stir until smooth. Set aside. In a large bowl, cream butter and brown sugar until light and fluffy. Add eggs, one at a time, beating well after each addition. Beat in vanilla and melted chocolate.

**2.** Combine the flour, baking soda, salt and baking powder; add to the creamed mixture alternately with the water and sour cream. Transfer to two greased and floured 9-in. round baking pans.

**3.** Bake at 350° for 25-30 minutes or until a toothpick inserted near the center comes out clean. Cool for 10 minutes before removing from pans to wire racks to cool completely.

**4.** For frosting, in a small heavy saucepan, melt butter and chocolate over low heat. Remove from the heat; cool for 5 minutes. In a large bowl, beat the confectioners' sugar, milk and vanilla until smooth. Gradually beat in chocolate mixture until frosting is light and fluffy. Spread between layers and over top and sides of cake. Refrigerate leftovers. **Yield:** 12 servings.

*Chocolate Temptation Brownies*

# Date Pudding Cake Loaf

*For old-fashioned appeal at Christmastime, try this moist cake baked in a loaf pan and dotted with chopped dates and walnuts. The recipe includes a homemade vanilla sauce.*
—*Nancy Foust, Stoneboro, Pennsylvania*

   1 cup finely chopped dates
   1 cup boiling water
4-1/2 teaspoons shortening
   1 cup sugar
   1 egg
   1 teaspoon vanilla extract
   1 cup all-purpose flour
   1 teaspoon baking soda
  1/2 teaspoon baking powder
   1 cup chopped walnuts
VANILLA SAUCE:
  1/2 cup sugar
  1/2 cup packed brown sugar
   1 tablespoon cornstarch
   1 cup milk
   1 teaspoon butter
   1 teaspoon vanilla extract

**1.** Place dates in a small bowl; add boiling water. Let stand for 5 minutes. Meanwhile, in a small bowl, beat shortening and sugar until crumbly, about 2 minutes. Add egg and vanilla; mix well. Combine the flour, baking soda and baking powder; add to shortening mixture alternately with dates and water. Fold in walnuts.

**2.** Transfer to a greased 9-in. x 5-in. loaf pan. Bake at 350° for 45-55 minutes or until a toothpick inserted near the center comes out clean. Cool on a wire rack for 20 minutes.

**3.** In a small saucepan, combine the sugars and cornstarch. Gradually whisk in milk until smooth. Bring to a boil over medium heat; cook and stir for 2 minutes or until thickened. Stir in butter and vanilla. Serve the sauce warm with cake. **Yield:** 12 servings (1-1/3 cups sauce).

# Chocolate Temptation Brownies

*Chocolate lovers will stand in line for these rich, three-layer squares that have a peanut butter filling and decadent glaze. They're heavenly!* —*Iola Egle, Bella Vista, Arkansas*

   1 cup butter, cubed
   1 ounce bittersweet chocolate, chopped
  3/4 cup sugar
  3/4 cup packed light brown sugar
   2 teaspoons vanilla extract
   3 eggs
1-1/4 cups all-purpose flour
  3/4 teaspoon salt
   1 cup chopped salted peanuts
PEANUT BUTTER FILLING:
  12 ounces cream cheese, softened
   1 cup creamy peanut butter
   1 cup confectioners' sugar
CHOCOLATE GLAZE:
   8 ounces bittersweet chocolate, finely chopped
  1/4 cup butter, cubed
  1/2 cup heavy whipping cream
  1/2 cup confectioners' sugar

**1.** In a large saucepan, melt butter and chocolate over medium heat. Remove from the heat; stir in sugars and vanilla. Add eggs, one at a time, stirring well after each addition. Combine flour and salt; stir into butter mixture just until combined. Stir in peanuts.

**2.** Transfer to a greased 13-in. x 9-in. baking pan. Bake at 350° for 25-30 minutes or until a toothpick inserted near the center comes out clean. Cool completely on a wire rack.

**3.** In a small bowl, beat the cream cheese, peanut butter and confectioners' sugar until light and fluffy; spread over brownie layer. Chill until firm.

**4.** In a microwave, melt chocolate and butter with cream; stir until smooth. Stir in confectioners' sugar. Spread over peanut butter layer. Chill until firm. **Yield:** 3 dozen.

*Pumpkin-Sweet Potato Pie with Sugared Pecans*

## Pumpkin-Sweet Potato Pie With Sugared Pecans

*This is not your typical pumpkin pie! With a smooth, creamy filling and pretty arrangement of nuts on top, it's an extra-special dessert.* —Loretta Lawrence, Myrtle Beach, South Carolina

    1 can (15 ounces) solid-pack pumpkin
    1 cup mashed sweet potatoes
    3/4 cup packed brown sugar
1-1/2 teaspoons ground cinnamon
    1/2 teaspoon salt
    1/2 teaspoon ground ginger
    1/2 teaspoon ground nutmeg
    1/4 teaspoon ground cloves
    3 eggs, beaten
1-1/4 cups heavy whipping cream
    1 can (5 ounces) evaporated milk
    1 tablespoon dark rum
Pastry for single-crust pie (9 inches)
PECANS:
    2 cups pecan halves
    1/2 cup packed brown sugar
    1/4 cup heavy whipping cream
Whipped cream

1. In a large bowl, combine the first eight ingredients. Add eggs, cream, milk and rum; mix well. Line a 9-in. deep-dish pie plate with pastry; trim and flute edges. Pour pumpkin mixture into pastry. Bake at 400° for 40-45 minutes or until a knife inserted near the center comes out clean. Cool on a wire rack.

2. In a small bowl, combine the pecans, brown sugar and cream. Spread into a greased 15-in. x 10-in. x 1-in. baking pan. Bake at 350° for 15-20 minutes or until toasted, stirring once. Cool completely.

3. Top pie with sugared pecans; serve with whipped cream. Refrigerate leftovers. **Yield:** 8 servings.

## Majestic Pecan Cake

*This recipe truly lives up to its name. The pecan-dotted cake is stacked in three layers, and made-from-scratch frosting is the crowning touch.* —Nancy Mueller, Menomonee Falls, Wisconsin

    1/2 cup butter, softened
    1/4 cup shortening
    2 cups sugar, *divided*
    2 teaspoons vanilla extract
    3 cups cake flour
    5 teaspoons baking powder
    1/2 teaspoon salt
1-1/3 cups whole milk
    6 egg whites
    1 cup chopped pecans
FILLING:
    1/3 cup sugar
    3 tablespoons cornstarch
    2 cups whole milk
    3 egg yolks, beaten
    1 tablespoon butter
1-1/2 teaspoons vanilla extract
FROSTING:
1-3/4 cups sugar
    4 egg whites
    1/2 cup water
    1/2 teaspoon cream of tartar
    1 teaspoon vanilla extract

1. Grease and flour three 9-in. round baking pans; set aside. In a large bowl, cream the butter, shortening and 1-3/4 cups sugar until light and fluffy. Beat in the vanilla. Combine the flour, baking powder and salt; add to the creamed mixture alternately with milk, beating well after each addition.

2. In a large bowl with clean beaters, beat egg whites until soft peaks form. Gradually beat in remaining sugar, 1 tablespoon at a time, on high until stiff peaks form. Fold into batter. Fold in nuts. Transfer to prepared pans. Bake at 350° for 18-22 minutes or until a toothpick inserted near the center comes out clean. Cool for 10 minutes before removing from pans to wire racks to cool completely.

3. For filling, in a small heavy saucepan, combine sugar and cornstarch; gradually stir in milk until smooth. Cook and stir over medium-high heat until thickened and bubbly. Reduce heat to low; cook and stir 2 minutes longer.

4. Remove from the heat. Stir a small amount of hot mixture into egg yolks; return all to the pan, stirring constantly. Bring to a gentle boil; cook and stir for 2 minutes. Remove from the heat; stir in butter and vanilla. Cool.

5. For frosting, in a large heavy saucepan, combine the sugar, egg whites, water and cream of tartar over low heat. With a hand mixer, beat on low speed for 1 minute. Continue beating on low over low heat until frosting reaches 160°, about 8-10 minutes. Pour into a large bowl; add vanilla. Beat on high until stiff peaks form, about 7 minutes.

6. Spread filling between cake layers. Frost cake. Store in the refrigerator. **Yield:** 16 servings.

Majestic Pecan Cake

Blueberry Colada Mini Loaves

*What makes eyes light up more than homemade treats from the kitchen?*
*Here, you'll find goodies to delight everyone on your Christmas list.*

# Blueberry Colada Mini Loaves

*What do you get when you combine a pina colada and quick bread? This delightfully different treat that mixes in plenty of blueberries, too. The recipe makes eight miniature loaves.*
*—Brenda Bonn, Geneva, Illinois*

2/3 cup shortening
1-1/3 cups sugar
4 eggs
1 can (8 ounces) crushed pineapple, drained
1/2 cup 2% milk
1-1/2 teaspoons lemon juice
3 cups all-purpose flour
2 teaspoons baking powder
1 teaspoon baking soda
1/2 teaspoon salt
2 cups fresh *or* frozen blueberries
1/2 cup flaked coconut

**1.** In a large bowl, cream the shortening and sugar until light and fluffy. Add the eggs, one at a time, beating well after each addition. Beat in the pineapple, milk and lemon juice. Combine the flour, baking powder, baking soda and salt; gradually beat into the creamed mixture. Fold in the blueberries and coconut.

**2.** Transfer to eight greased 4-1/2-in. x 2-1/2-in. x 1-1/2-in. loaf pans. Bake at 350° for 25-30 minutes or until a toothpick inserted near the center comes out clean.

**3.** Cool for 15 minutes before removing from pans to wire racks. **Yield:** 8 mini loaves (6 slices each).

**Editor's Note:** If using frozen blueberries, use without thawing to avoid discoloring the batter.

# Holiday Cheese Balls

*I received this party-perfect recipe from the wife of one of my co-workers. Everyone loves the delicious yet simple blend of cheeses, Worcestershire sauce, onions, parsley and pecans.*
*—Carol Hawley, Frederick, Maryland*

4 packages (3 ounces *each*) cream cheese, softened
1-1/2 cups (6 ounces) crumbled blue cheese
1 cup process cheese sauce
1 cup finely chopped pecans, *divided*
1/2 cup minced fresh parsley, *divided*
2 tablespoons finely chopped onion
1 teaspoon Worcestershire sauce
Assorted crackers

**1.** In a large bowl, combine the cream cheese, blue cheese and cheese sauce. Add 1/2 cup pecans, 1/4 cup parsley, onion and Worcestershire sauce; mix well. Cover and refrigerate for 2 hours.

**2.** Shape into two balls. Combine the remaining pecans and parsley; roll cheese balls in pecan mixture. Wrap in plastic wrap; refrigerate for at least 1 hour. Serve with crackers. **Yield:** 2 cheese balls (1-3/4 cups each).

# Pumpkin Pie Coffee Creamer

*Anyone who likes a cup of java is sure to enjoy this homemade stir-in. For a quick Christmas gift, put the creamer in a festive basket and add a fun mug or package of gourmet coffee.*
*—Carol Forcum, Marion, Illinois*

1 cup powdered nondairy creamer
4 teaspoons ground cinnamon
2 teaspoons ground ginger
2 teaspoons ground nutmeg
1 teaspoon ground cloves
1 teaspoon ground allspice

In a small bowl, combine all ingredients. Store in an airtight container. **Yield:** about 1 cup.

*Pumpkin Pie Coffee Creamer*

# Christmas Bears Snack Mix

*This sweet-salty finger food is perfect for packing in holiday bags to give as gifts or stocking stuffers. Plus, you'll need just moments to make it.* —Joan Hallford, North Richland Hills, Texas

    4 cups popped popcorn
    2 cups chocolate bear-shaped crackers
    2 cups miniature cream-filled chocolate sandwich
        cookies
    2 cups red and green milk chocolate M&M's
    1 cup red and green gummy bears

In a large bowl, combine all ingredients. Store in an airtight container. **Yield:** about 2-1/2 quarts.

# Carrot Cake Jam

*For a change of pace from berry jams, try this unique option. Spread on a bagel with cream cheese, it tastes almost as good as real carrot cake!* —Rachelle Stratton, Rock Springs, Wyoming

    1 can (20 ounces) unsweetened crushed pineapple,
        undrained
1-1/2 cups shredded carrots
1-1/2 cups chopped peeled ripe pears
    3 tablespoons lemon juice
    1 teaspoon ground cinnamon
    1/4 teaspoon ground cloves
    1/4 teaspoon ground nutmeg
    1 package (1-3/4 ounces) powdered fruit pectin
6-1/2 cups sugar

**1.** In a large saucepan, combine the first seven ingredients. Bring to a boil. Reduce heat; cover and simmer for 15-20 minutes or until pears are tender, stirring occasionally. Remove from the heat; stir in pectin.

*Carrot Cake Jam*

**2.** Bring mixture to a full rolling boil over high heat, stirring constantly. Stir in sugar; return to a full rolling boil. Boil for 1 minute, stirring constantly. Remove from the heat; skim off foam.

**3.** Ladle the hot mixture into hot sterilized half-pint jars, leaving 1/4-in. headspace. Remove air bubbles; wipe rims and adjust lids. Process in a boiling-water canner for 5 minutes. **Yield:** 8 half-pints.

# Caramel Chex Mix

*This crunchy, nutty snack has mass appeal. Make it during the Christmas season or whenever your family is craving something yummy to munch.* —Rose Marie Domeny, Mundelein, Illinois

    6 cups Crispix
    6 cups Rice Chex
    6 cups Corn Chex
    3 cups Wheat Chex
    1 pound dry roasted peanuts
2-1/4 cups packed brown sugar
    1 cup butter, cubed
    1/2 cup light corn syrup
    1 tablespoon vanilla extract

**1.** In a greased roasting pan, combine cereals and peanuts; set aside. In a large heavy saucepan, combine the brown sugar, butter and corn syrup. Bring to a boil, stirring constantly. Boil for 5 minutes, stirring occasionally. Remove from the heat; stir in vanilla. Pour over cereal mixture and stir to coat.

**2.** Bake at 250° for 1 hour, stirring every 15 minutes. Cool. Store in an airtight container. **Yield:** 7 quarts.

# Chocolate Gingerbread Cookie Mix

*Satisfy gingerbread fans and chocoholics alike with a merry gift of cookie mix in a festive tin. They can cut the rolled dough into any shapes they like.* —Redawna Kalynchuk, Sexsmith, Alberta

2-1/2 cups all-purpose flour
    2/3 cup sugar
    1 teaspoon ground ginger
    1/2 teaspoon baking soda
    1/4 teaspoon salt
    1/4 teaspoon ground nutmeg
1-1/2 cups semisweet chocolate chips
**ADDITIONAL INGREDIENTS:**
    1/2 cup butter, cubed
    1/2 cup molasses
    1/4 cup water

**1.** In a large bowl, combine the first six ingredients. Transfer to a resealable plastic bag. Place chips in a resealable plastic bag. Place both bags in a cookie tin. **Yield:** 1 batch.

**2. To prepare cookies:** In a large saucepan, combine the chips, butter, molasses and water. Cook and stir over low heat until the chips and butter are melted. Remove from the heat. Stir in the dry ingredients to form a soft dough. Transfer the dough to a bowl; cover and refrigerate for 2 hours or until easy to handle.

**3.** On a lightly floured surface, roll dough to 1/4-in. thickness. Cut with a floured 3-1/2-in. gingerbread cookie cutter. Place 2 in. apart on ungreased baking sheets. Reroll scraps. Bake at 375° for 8-10 minutes or until set. Cool for 1-2 minutes before removing from pans to wire racks. **Yield:** 3 dozen.

# Jalapeno-Pear Chutney

*With tongue-tingling peppers, pears, tomatoes and more, this versatile chutney is a mouthful of flavor. Serve it alongside your favorite meat entree…as a sandwich spread…over cream cheese for an appetizer…or even with chips as a salsa-style dip.*
— *Deb Thomson, Grand Island, Nebraska*

   2 pounds pears, peeled and chopped
   2 pounds tomatoes, peeled, seeded and chopped
   2 cups chopped onions
   1 cup finely chopped seeded jalapeno peppers
   1 cup cider vinegar
   1 cup packed brown sugar
   4 teaspoons minced fresh gingerroot
   1 to 2 teaspoons crushed red pepper flakes
   1 teaspoon ground mustard

**1.** In a Dutch oven, combine all ingredients. Bring to a boil. Reduce heat; simmer, uncovered, for 45-60 minutes or until thickened, stirring occasionally.

**2.** Carefully ladle hot mixture into hot half-pint jars, leaving 1/2-in. headspace. Remove air bubbles; wipe rims and adjust lids. Process for 10 minutes in a boiling-water canner. **Yield:** 5 half-pints.

**Editor's Note:** When cutting hot peppers, disposable gloves are recommended. Avoid touching your face.

# Sesame Cheese Crackers

*These tasty homemade crackers are irresistible! Enjoy them with soups, or munch on them all by themselves. Cayenne pepper adds a bit of a kick.* — *Margaret Inlow, Joliet, Illinois*

   1 cup all-purpose flour
1/2 teaspoon salt
1/8 to 1/4 teaspoon cayenne pepper
   6 tablespoons cold butter
   1 cup (4 ounces) finely shredded cheddar cheese
1/4 cup sesame seeds, toasted
   6 to 7-1/2 teaspoons ice water, *divided*
1/2 teaspoon soy sauce

**1.** In a small bowl, combine the flour, salt and cayenne; cut in butter until mixture resembles coarse crumbs. Stir in cheese and sesame seeds. Combine 3 teaspoons ice water and soy sauce; stir into dry ingredients with a fork. Stir in enough remaining water until dough forms a ball. Wrap tightly in plastic wrap; refrigerate for 1 hour or until firm.

*Sesame Cheese Crackers*

**2.** On a floured surface, roll dough into a 14-in. x 11-in. rectangle. Cut into 2-in. x 1-in. strips. Place on lightly greased baking sheets. Bake at 400° for 12-15 minutes or until golden brown. Remove to wire racks to cool. **Yield:** 77 crackers.

# Toffee Biscotti

*A traditional Italian cookie that is baked twice, biscotti is ideal for dunking. Feel free to use any toffee candy bar you like for this recipe.* — *LilRedHen, Taste of Home Online Community*

   3 eggs
1/2 cup canola oil
1/2 cup sugar
1/4 cup packed brown sugar
   2 teaspoons vanilla extract
   3 cups all-purpose flour
   2 teaspoons baking powder
Dash salt
   5 Heath candy bars (1.4 ounces *each*), chopped
1/2 cup pecan halves

**1.** In a large bowl, beat the eggs, oil, sugars and vanilla. Combine the flour, baking powder and salt; gradually add to sugar mixture and mix well. Stir in candy and pecans (dough will be sticky).

**2.** Divide dough in half. With lightly floured hands, shape each half on a greased baking sheet into a 12-in. x 3-in. rectangle. Bake at 350° for 25-30 minutes or until golden brown.

**3.** Carefully remove to wire racks; cool for 15 minutes. Transfer to a cutting board; cut diagonally with a serrated knife into 3/4-in. slices. Place cut side down on parchment paper-lined baking sheets.

**4.** Bake for 15 minutes or until firm. Turn and bake 5-7 minutes longer or until lightly browned. Remove to wire racks to cool. Store in an airtight container. **Yield:** 2-1/2 dozen.

Hazelnut Shortbread Hearts

## Hazelnut Shortbread Hearts

*Toasted hazelnuts add a nice crunch and flavor to these rich, buttery hearts. The drizzle of dark and white chocolate gives the cookies an impressive look, but they couldn't be easier to make.*
—Monique Theoret, Wooster, Ohio

1-1/2 cups butter, softened
   1 cup confectioners' sugar
   3 teaspoons vanilla extract
   3 cups all-purpose flour
   1 cup ground toasted hazelnuts
   4 ounces bittersweet chocolate, melted
   2 ounces white baking chocolate, melted

**1.** In a large bowl, cream butter and confectioners' sugar until light and fluffy. Stir in vanilla. Combine flour and hazelnuts; gradually add to creamed mixture and mix well. Cover and refrigerate for 1 hour or until easy to handle.

**2.** On a lightly floured surface, roll out dough to 1/4-in. thickness. Cut with a floured 2-in. heart-shaped cookie cutter. Place 1 in. apart on ungreased baking sheets.

**3.** Bake at 325° for 18-20 minutes or until lightly browned. Cool for 1 minute before removing from pans to wire racks to cool completely.

**4.** Drizzle chocolate over cookies; let stand until set. Store in an airtight container. **Yield:** 7-1/2 dozen.

## Chocolate Amaretti

*With a hint of almond, these chewy treats are similar to those sold in Italian bakeries. My husband and children are always excited when I include these in my holiday baking lineup.*
—Kathy Long, Whitefish Bay, Wisconsin

1-1/4 cups almond paste
   3/4 cup sugar
   2 egg whites
   1/2 cup confectioners' sugar
   1/4 cup baking cocoa

**1.** In a large bowl, beat the almond paste, sugar and egg whites until combined. Combine confectioners' sugar and cocoa; gradually add to almond mixture and mix well.

**2.** Drop dough by tablespoonfuls 2 in. apart onto parchment paper-lined baking sheets. Bake at 350° for 17-20 minutes or until tops are cracked. Cool for 1 minute before removing from pans to wire racks. Store in an airtight container. **Yield:** 3 dozen.

## Chocolate Mexican Wedding Cakes

*These spiced balls are a yummy twist on a traditional favorite. Sometimes I add mini chocolate chips to the dough and, after baking, dip the cooled cookies in melted almond bark.*
—Joanne Valkema, Freeport, Illinois

   1 cup butter, softened
1-3/4 cups confectioners' sugar, *divided*
   1 teaspoon vanilla extract
1-1/2 cups all-purpose flour
   1/4 cup cornstarch
   1/4 cup baking cocoa
   1/2 teaspoon salt
1-1/4 cups finely chopped pecans *or* almonds
   1/2 teaspoon ground cinnamon

**1.** In a large bowl, cream butter and 1 cup confectioners' sugar until light and fluffy. Beat in vanilla. Combine the flour, cornstarch, cocoa and salt; gradually add to creamed mixture and mix well. Stir in nuts.

**2.** Shape tablespoonfuls of dough into 1-in. balls. Place 2 in. apart on ungreased baking sheets. Bake at 325° for 12-14 minutes or until set.

**3.** In a small bowl, combine cinnamon and remaining sugar. Roll the warm cookies in sugar mixture; cool on wire racks. Store in an airtight container. **Yield:** about 3-1/2 dozen.

*Chocolate Mexican Wedding Cakes*

# Cranberry-Pistachio Cookie Cups

*If you're looking for something special to add to your holiday dessert tray, try these little shortbread-like cups. They're easy to make and have a delightful fruit-and-nut center.*
—*Betty Claycomb, Alverton, Pennsylvania*

   1/2 cup butter, softened
     1 package (3 ounces) cream cheese, softened
     2 tablespoons sugar
   1/2 teaspoon grated orange peel
     1 cup all-purpose flour
**FILLING:**
     1 egg
     1 cup confectioners' sugar
     1 tablespoon butter, melted
   1/2 cup pistachios, chopped
   1/3 cup dried cranberries

**1.** In a large bowl, cream the butter, cream cheese, sugar and orange peel until light and fluffy. Add flour; mix well. Cover and refrigerate for 1 hour or until easy to handle.

**2.** In a small bowl, combine the egg, confectioners' sugar and butter. Stir in pistachios and cranberries. Shape the dough into 24 balls. Press onto the bottom and up the sides of ungreased miniature muffin cups. Spoon filling into cups.

**3.** Bake cups at 350° for 20-25 minutes or until set. Cool for 10 minutes before removing from pans to wire racks to cool completely. Store in an airtight container. **Yield:** 2 dozen.

*Cranberry-Pistachio Cookie Cups*

# Just-Like-Pecan-Pie Bars

*With a rich, butter crust and chewy nut filling, these bars are just as good as real pecan pie! Cut them in pretty triangle or diamond shapes.*
—*Judie Heiderscheit, Holy Cross, Iowa*

     2 cups all-purpose flour
   1/4 cup sugar
   1/2 teaspoon salt
   1/2 teaspoon baking powder
     1 cup cold butter
**FILLING:**
 1-1/4 cups packed brown sugar
     1 cup butter, cubed
   3/4 cup honey
   1/2 cup sugar
     4 cups chopped pecans
   1/4 cup heavy whipping cream
     3 teaspoons vanilla extract

**1.** Line a 13-in. x 9-in. baking pan with foil; coat the foil with cooking spray and set aside.

**2.** In a large bowl, combine the flour, sugar, salt and baking powder. Cut in butter until mixture resembles coarse crumbs. Press into prepared pan. Bake at 350° for 20-25 minutes or until golden brown.

**3.** Meanwhile, in a large saucepan, combine brown sugar, butter, honey and sugar. Bring to a boil over medium heat; cook and stir for 3 minutes. Remove from the heat; stir in the pecans, cream and vanilla. Pour over the crust. Bake 30 minutes longer or until filling is bubbly.

**4.** Cool on a wire rack. Use foil to lift bars out of pan. Place on a cutting board; carefully remove foil. Cut into 32 bars; cut each in half diagonally. **Yield:** 64 bars.

# Frosted Anise Sugar Cookies

(Pictured on page 67)

*These soft, cake-like cookies have a pleasant anise flavor that's distinct but not overpowering. I add red and green sprinkles for Christmas, but you could decorate them to suit any occasion.*
—*Janice Eanni, Willowick, Ohio*

     1 cup butter, softened
 1-1/2 cups sugar
     6 eggs
     1 teaspoon vanilla extract
   3/4 teaspoon anise extract
 3-1/2 cups all-purpose flour
     4 teaspoons baking powder
**ICING:**
     4 cups confectioners' sugar
     2 tablespoons butter, softened
     1 teaspoon vanilla extract
     2 to 4 tablespoons milk
Colored sprinkles, optional

**1.** In a large bowl, cream butter and sugar until light and fluffy. Beat in eggs and extracts. Combine flour and baking powder; gradually add to creamed mixture and mix well.

**2.** Drop by tablespoonfuls 2 in. apart onto greased baking sheets. Bake at 350° for 8-10 minutes or until lightly browned. Remove to wire racks to cool completely.

**3.** For icing, in a large bowl, combine the confectioners' sugar, butter, vanilla and enough milk to achieve spreading consistency. Frost cookies; place on waxed paper. Decorate with sprinkles if desired; let stand until set. Store in an airtight container. **Yield:** 7 dozen.

## Coconut-Pecan Shortbread Cookies

(Pictured on page 67)

*Similar to linzer cookies, these shortbread treats have a luscious caramel filling. They take a little bit of time to make but are well worth it.* —Cathy Grubelnick, Raton, New Mexico

   1 cup butter, softened
1/2 cup sugar
   1 teaspoon vanilla extract
   2 cups all-purpose flour
1/2 teaspoon salt
1/2 cup flaked coconut
1/2 cup chopped pecans
FILLING:
2/3 cup sugar
   3 tablespoons water
   1 teaspoon light corn syrup
1/4 cup heavy whipping cream
   2 tablespoons butter

**1.** In a large bowl, cream butter and sugar until light and fluffy. Beat in vanilla. Combine flour and salt; gradually add to creamed mixture and mix well. Stir in coconut and pecans. Divide dough into two portions. Cover and refrigerate for 30 minutes or until easy to handle.

**2.** On a floured surface, roll each portion to 1/8-in. thickness. Cut with a 1-in round cookie cutter. Place 1 in. apart on greased baking sheets. Bake at 350° for 10-12 minutes or until lightly browned. Cool for 1 minute before removing from pans to wire racks to cool completely.

**3.** Meanwhile, for filling, in a large heavy saucepan, bring sugar and water to a boil. Add corn syrup; cook until syrup turns golden, about 5 minutes (do not stir). Gradually stir in cream and butter.

**4.** Spread 1/2 teaspoon caramel filling on the bottoms of half of the cookies; top with remaining cookies. Let stand for 2 hours or until set. **Yield:** 4 dozen.

## Good Fortune & Cheer Cookies

*You'll love stuffing Christmas greetings and well wishes into these fun homemade cookies—and your family and friends will love receiving them!* —Beverly Preston, Fond du Lac, Wisconsin

   6 tablespoons butter, softened
1/3 cup sugar

*Good Fortune & Cheer Cookies*

   2 egg whites
1/2 teaspoon vanilla extract
1/2 teaspoon rum extract
2/3 cup all-purpose flour
   3 ounces white baking chocolate, chopped
Crushed peppermint candies
Red, white and green nonpareils

**1.** Write fortunes on small strips of paper (3 in. x 1/2 in.); set aside. Using a pencil, draw two 3-in. circles on a sheet of parchment paper. Place sheet, pencil mark down, on a baking sheet; set aside.

**2.** In a large bowl, beat the butter, sugar, egg whites and extracts until well blended. Add flour; mix well (batter will be thick). Spread a scant tablespoonful of batter over each circle. Bake at 400° for 5-6 minutes or until edges are lightly browned.

**3.** Slide parchment paper onto a work surface. Cover one cookie with a kitchen towel to keep warm. Place a fortune in the center of the other cookie; loosen cookie from parchment paper with a thin spatula. Fold cookie in half over fortune so the edges meet.

**4.** Place center of cookie over the rim of a glass; gently press ends down to bend cookie. Cool for 1 minute before removing to a wire rack. Repeat with second cookie. If cookies become too cool to fold, return to oven to soften for 1 minute. Repeat with remaining batter and fortunes.

**5.** In a microwave, melt chocolate; stir until smooth. Partially dip cookies or drizzle as desired; place on waxed paper. Sprinkle with crushed candies and nonpareils. Let stand until set. Store in an airtight container. **Yield:** 1-1/2 dozen.

Peppermint Stick Cookies

# Peppermint Stick Cookies

*With cool mint flavor and a festive look, these whimsical creations will make you feel like you're in the North Pole. The chilled dough is easy to shape, too.* —Nancy Knapke, Fort Recovery, Ohio

    1 cup unsalted butter, softened
    1 cup sugar
    1 egg
    2 teaspoons mint extract
    1/2 teaspoon vanilla extract
  2-3/4 cups all-purpose flour
    1/2 teaspoon salt
    12 drops red food coloring
    12 drops green food coloring
  1-1/2 cups white baking chips
Crushed mint candies

**1.** In a large bowl, cream butter and sugar until light and fluffy. Beat in egg and extracts. Combine flour and salt; gradually add to the creamed mixture and mix well.

**2.** Set aside half of the dough. Divide remaining dough in half; add red food coloring to one portion and green food coloring to the other. Wrap dough separately in plastic wrap. Refrigerate for 1-2 hours or until easy to handle.

**3.** Divide the green and red dough into 24 portions each. Divide plain dough into 48 portions. Roll each into a 4-in. rope. Place each green rope next to a plain rope; press together gently and twist. Repeat with red ropes and remaining plain ropes. Place 2 in. apart on ungreased baking sheets.

**4.** Bake at 350° for 10-12 minutes or until set. Cool for 2 minutes before carefully removing from the pans to wire racks to cool completely.

**5.** In a microwave, melt chips; stir until smooth. Dip cookie ends into melted chips; allow excess to drip off. Sprinkle with candies and place on waxed paper. Let stand until set. Store in an airtight container. **Yield: 4 dozen.**

# Raspberry Thumbprints

*Berry jam really complements these tender, buttery treats rolled in nuts. With a ruby-red center, they're especially nice for the holiday season.* —Linda Harrington, Hudson, New Hampshire

    1/2 cup butter, softened
    1/4 cup packed brown sugar
    1 egg, *separated*
    1/2 teaspoon vanilla extract
    1 cup all-purpose flour
    1/4 teaspoon salt
    3/4 cup finely chopped walnuts
    1/2 cup seedless raspberry *or* strawberry jam

**1.** In a small bowl, cream butter and brown sugar until light and fluffy. Beat in egg yolk and vanilla. Combine flour and salt; gradually add to creamed mixture. Cover and refrigerate for 1 hour or until dough is easy to handle.

**2.** In a shallow bowl, whisk egg white until foamy. Place nuts in another shallow bowl. Shape dough into 3/4-in. balls. Dip in egg white, then roll in nuts.

**3.** Place 1 in. apart on ungreased baking sheets. Using a wooden spoon handle, make an indentation in the center of each cookie. Bake at 350° for 8-10 minutes or until set.

**4,** Remove to wire racks to cool completely. Spoon jam into each cookie. Store in an airtight container. **Yield: 3 dozen.**

# Chocolate Peanut Butter Thumbprints

*The popular combination of chocolate and peanut butter is hard to beat...and the cream filling in these cookies takes them beyond the ordinary!* —Nancy Foust, Stoneboro, Pennsylvania

    1 cup butter-flavored shortening
    1 cup sugar
    2 egg yolks
    2 tablespoons milk
    2 ounces unsweetened chocolate, melted and cooled
    1 teaspoon vanilla extract
    2 cups all-purpose flour
    1/2 teaspoon salt
    2/3 cup miniature semisweet chocolate chips
FILLING:
    1/3 cup creamy peanut butter
    2 tablespoons butter-flavored shortening
    1 cup plus 2 tablespoons confectioners' sugar
    2 tablespoons milk
    1/2 teaspoon vanilla extract

**1.** In a large bowl, cream shortening and sugar. Beat in the egg yolks, milk, melted chocolate and vanilla. Combine flour and salt; gradually add to chocolate mixture. Stir in chocolate chips. Roll into 1-in. balls.

**2.** Place 2 in. apart on greased baking sheets. Using the end of a wooden spoon handle, make an indentation in the center of each ball. Bake at 350° for 11-13 minutes or until firm. Remove to wire racks to cool completely.

**3.** Meanwhile, for filling, in a small bowl, beat peanut butter and shortening until combined. Beat in the confectioners' sugar, milk and vanilla until smooth. Fill cookies with filling. Store in an airtight container. **Yield: about 3 dozen.**

*Chocolate Peanut Butter Thumbprints*
*Frosted Anise Sugar Cookies (p. 64)*
*Coconut-Pecan Shortbread Cookies (p. 65)*

*Cherry Cordials*
*Les Truffles Au Chocolat*

# Cherry Cordials

*This Christmas, skip the boxed chocolate-covered cherries sitting on store shelves. The taste of these homemade confections just can't be beat. Plus, they're a snap to make with only three basic ingredients—you simply soak the cherries in brandy, melt the chocolate and dip!* —Dorothy Bayard, Hubertus, Wisconsin

    1 jar (10 ounces) maraschino cherries with stems, drained
    1/2 cup brandy
    1 cup (6 ounces) semisweet chocolate chips

**1.** Place cherries in a small bowl; add brandy. Cover and freeze for at least 3 hours.

**2.** Place chocolate chips in a small heavy saucepan. Cook over low heat until chips begin to melt. Remove from the heat; stir. Return to the heat; cook just until melted. Immediately remove from the heat; stir until smooth.

**3.** Pat the cherries dry. Holding onto the stems, dip cherries into chocolate; allow excess to drip off. Place on a waxed paper-lined pan. Refrigerate for 10 minutes or until firm. Store in an airtight container in the refrigerator. **Yield:** about 2 dozen.

# Les Truffles Au Chocolat

*These decadent dipped balls have the wonderful combination of chocolate and orange. If it's more convenient, make them a day ahead of time and store them in the fridge overnight to chill.* —Sally Gregg, Twinsburg, Ohio

    1 cup (6 ounces) semisweet chocolate chips
    1 cup (6 ounces) milk chocolate chips
    5 tablespoons butter, cubed
    1 cup plus 2 tablespoons confectioners' sugar
    3 tablespoons heavy whipping cream
    3 tablespoons thawed orange juice concentrate
    1 teaspoon vanilla extract
    3 tablespoons baking cocoa

**1.** In a small heavy saucepan, combine the chocolate chips and butter. Cook and stir over low heat until melted and smooth. Remove from the heat. Stir in the confectioners' sugar, cream, orange juice concentrate and vanilla. Cover and refrigerate for 3 hours or until firm.

**2.** Working quickly, shape mixture into 1-in. balls; roll in cocoa. Store in an airtight container in the refrigerator. **Yield:** 3 dozen.

# Crunchy Peanut Butter Candy

*Anyone who likes peanuts will love this sweet treat that's packed full of them. After breaking the pan of cooled candy into pieces, I finish with a simple but festive drizzle of melted chocolate.* —Connie Pietila, Houghton, Michigan

    1-1/2 teaspoons butter
    2-1/2 cups creamy peanut butter
    2 cups salted peanuts
    1/2 teaspoon vanilla extract
    2 cups sugar
    1-1/2 cups light corn syrup
    1/4 cup water
    1-1/2 teaspoons baking soda
    1/2 cup semisweet chocolate chips

**1.** Grease a 15-in. x 10-in. x 1-in. pan with butter; set aside. Combine the peanut butter, peanuts and vanilla; set aside.

**2.** In a large heavy saucepan, combine the sugar, corn syrup and water; bring to a boil over medium heat, stirring constantly. Cook, without stirring, until a candy thermometer reads 300° (hard-crack stage). Immediately stir in peanut butter mixture and baking soda. Spread into prepared pan. Cool completely.

**3.** Break candy into pieces. Melt chocolate chips; stir until smooth. Drizzle over candy. Store in an airtight container. **Yield:** 3-1/2 pounds.

**Editor's Note:** We recommend that you test your candy thermometer before each use by bringing water to a boil; the thermometer should read 212°. Adjust your recipe temperature up or down based on your test.

*Crunchy Peanut Butter Candy*

# Holiday Marshmallows

*These soft homemade marshmallows are lots more fun than the store-bought kind and so yummy, whether by themselves or topping off a mug of hot cocoa. I add red and green sprinkles for the holidays.* —Arlene Barr, Monterey, California

        2 teaspoons butter
        1 package (3 ounces) strawberry gelatin
    1/2 cup water
    3/4 cup sugar
        3 tablespoons light corn syrup
Assorted sprinkles, confectioners' sugar, coarse colored
    sugar *and/or* nonpareils

1. Line an 8-in. square pan with foil and lightly grease the foil with 2 teaspoons butter; set aside.

2. In a small saucepan, combine gelatin and water. Cook and stir over medium-low heat until gelatin is dissolved. Add sugar and corn syrup; cook and stir until sugar is dissolved (do not boil).

3. Transfer to a large bowl. Chill until slightly thickened, about 30 minutes. Beat on high speed until mixture is thick and the volume is doubled, about 10 minutes. Spread into prepared pan. Cover and refrigerate for 6 hours or overnight.

4. Using foil, lift the marshmallows out of pan. Cut into 1-1/4-in. squares or cut into shapes with cutters lightly coated with cooking spray. Roll in sprinkles, sugar or nonpareils as desired. Store in an airtight container in a cool dry place. **Yield:** about 3 dozen.

*Holiday Marshmallows*

# Cherry Divinity

*It's just not Christmas without these light and airy confections on my dessert platter. The recipe is versatile because you can replace the cherry gelatin with any flavor that suits your taste.* —Crystal Ralph-Haughn, Bartlesville, Oklahoma

        2 egg whites
        3 cups sugar
    3/4 cup water
    3/4 cup light corn syrup
        1 package (3 ounces) cherry gelatin
        1 cup chopped walnuts

1. Place egg whites in a large stand mixer bowl; let stand at room temperature for 30 minutes.

2. In a heavy saucepan, combine the sugar, water and corn syrup; cook and stir until sugar is dissolved and mixture comes to a boil. Cook over medium heat, without stirring, until a candy thermometer reads 250° (hard-ball stage).

3. Just before the temperature is reached, beat egg whites until foamy. Gradually beat in gelatin. Beat until stiff peaks form. With mixer running on high speed, carefully pour hot syrup in a slow, steady stream into the bowl. Beat just until candy loses its gloss and holds its shape, about 5 minutes. Immediately stir in walnuts.

4. Quickly drop by tablespoonfuls onto waxed paper. Let stand at room temperature overnight or until dry to the touch. Store candy in an airtight container at room temperature. **Yield:** 5 dozen.

**Editor's Note:** We recommend that you test your candy thermometer before each use by bringing water to a boil; the thermometer should read 212°. Adjust your recipe temperature up or down based on your test.

# Molasses Taffy

*For an old-fashioned treat that's sure to get smiles from guests of all ages, try these individually wrapped squares of chocolaty taffy. Yum!* —Suzan Wiener, Spring Hill, Florida

        1 teaspoon plus 3 tablespoons butter, *divided*
        1 cup sugar
        1 cup water
        1 cup molasses
        2 ounces unsweetened chocolate, chopped
    1-1/2 teaspoons vanilla extract

1. Line an 8-in. square pan with foil. Grease the foil with 1 teaspoon butter; set aside.

2. In a large heavy saucepan, combine the sugar, water, molasses and remaining butter. Bring to a boil, stirring constantly. Cook without stirring until a candy thermometer reads 260° (hard-ball stage).

3. Remove from the heat; stir in chocolate and vanilla. Pour into prepared pan. Cool slightly. Score the surface into small squares. Cool completely and cut along the scored lines.

Wrap candy in waxed paper. Store in an airtight container. **Yield:** 1 pound.

**Editor's Note:** We recommend that you test your candy thermometer before each use by bringing water to a boil; the thermometer should read 212°. Adjust your recipe temperature up or down based on your test.

# Cherry Walnut Fudge

*Fudge lovers will rave about this confection from the country cooks in our Test Kitchen. The rich squares are loaded with dried cherries, chopped walnuts and a hint of almond.*

    3 tablespoons butter, *divided*
    2 cups (12 ounces) dark chocolate chips
    2 cups (12 ounces) semisweet chocolate chips
    1 jar (7 ounces) marshmallow creme
 4-1/2 cups sugar
    1 can (12 ounces) evaporated milk
    2 cups chopped walnuts
    2 cups dried cherries
    1 teaspoon vanilla extract
 1/2 teaspoon almond extract

**1.** Line a 13-in. x 9-in. pan with foil; butter foil with 1 tablespoon butter and set aside. Place the chocolate chips and marshmallow creme in a large bowl; set aside.

**2.** In a large saucepan, bring the sugar, milk and remaining butter to a boil over medium heat, stirring often. Reduce heat; simmer, uncovered, for 6 minutes, stirring occasionally. Slowly pour over chocolate mixture; stir until smooth. Stir in the walnuts, cherries and extracts.

**3.** Pour into prepared pan. Let stand at room temperature until cool. Using foil, lift fudge out of pan. Gently peel off foil; cut fudge into 1-in. squares. Store in an airtight container in the refrigerator. **Yield:** 3 pounds.

# Caramel Nougat Candy

*With crunchy peanuts, gooey caramel and fluffy marshmallow creme, these sweet sensations taste just like one of my favorite candy bars. I usually make several batches of candy at a time to include on my Christmas dessert tray or to give as gifts.*
—*Maddymoo, Taste of Home Online Community*

    8 ounces white baking chocolate, chopped
 1/2 cup marshmallow creme
 1/2 cup creamy peanut butter
    1 package (14 ounces) caramels
    1 tablespoon water
 1-1/2 cups chopped salted peanuts

**1.** In a large microwave-safe bowl, melt white chocolate; stir until smooth. Stir in marshmallow creme and peanut butter. Let stand 5 minutes or until cool enough to handle. Roll into 3/4-in. balls.

**2.** In another microwave-safe bowl, melt caramels with water; stir until smooth. Dip balls in caramel; allow excess to

*Caramel Nougat Candy*

drip off. Roll in peanuts and place on waxed paper-lined baking sheets. Chill until firm. Store in an airtight container in the refrigerator. **Yield:** 4 dozen.

**Editor's Note:** This recipe was tested in a 1,100-watt microwave.

# Benne Candy

*I love anything that has sesame seeds. This hard candy is a cinch to make with the inexpensive, pre-toasted seeds sold at Asian grocery stores. Plus, you'll need only four other ingredients.*
—*Lillian Julow, Gainesville, Florida*

    2 teaspoons plus 2 tablespoons butter, *divided*
 2-1/3 cups packed brown sugar
 1/2 cup milk
    1 tablespoon white vinegar
    1 cup sesame seeds, toasted

**1.** Grease a baking sheet with 2 teaspoons butter; set aside. In a small heavy saucepan, combine the brown sugar, milk, vinegar and remaining butter. Cook and stir over medium heat until a candy thermometer reads 280° (soft-crack stage). Remove from the heat; stir in sesame seeds.

**2.** Immediately pour onto prepared pan; spread into a 12-in. x 9-in. rectangle. Using a sharp knife, score warm candy into 1-1/2-in. squares (do not cut through). Cool completely; break into pieces along scored lines. Store in an airtight container. **Yield:** 1-1/4 pounds.

**Editor's Note:** We recommend that you test your candy thermometer before each use by bringing water to a boil; the thermometer should read 212°. Adjust your recipe temperature up or down based on your test.

# A Mother's Letter to Santa Claus

*Georgia Mueller, Charlottesville, Virginia*

My children all have written you
With lists of games and toys
And promises that they'll be
Well-behaved young girls and boys

Now may a mother say a word
For some things she desires?
Or even more, what she does not?
For repetition tires

Oh please, sir, no more pots and pans
You've brought me those before
Of kitchen gadgets I have lots
From Christmases of yore

No aprons, towels, tablecloths
(I've seen enough of those)
But I would never be averse
To having some new clothes

A ruffled nightgown would be nice
And slippers with a bow
A pretty sweater in pastels
Would set my face aglow

If those are not directions
Where your inclination leads
I'd also be delighted with
Some shiny pearls or beads

Although I treasure motherhood
And fondly do my part
Don't blame me if on Christmas Day
I'm still a girl at heart.

# Snowscape

*Marie Savage, Youngstown, Ohio*

The clouds shake snow upon the land

To paint, as by an artist's hand

A winter landscape pure and bright

To hail this lovely Christmas night

And when we rise to greet the day

All nature's artists seem to say

We've given you from up above

A setting for this time of love.

Grace your table with a
*Christmas Chapel*

WHAT A DIVINE IDEA—gingerbread dough baked and shaped to resemble a quaint country church at Christmas!

The country women in our Test Kitchen created a cheery chapel that's a sweet change of pace from the usual gingerbread house. Your holiday guests are sure to praise this awe-inspiring decoration when they see it in all its glory.

From the beautiful stained glass windows and red roof dusted with "snow" to the wreath-adorned doors and green shrubs, the delightful details on this house of worship are truly heavenly. And the best part is, it's not difficult to make!

Our Test Kitchen has provided the recipe, how-to photos and patterns beginning below. Follow these directions, and you'll soon have a special confection full of seasonal spirit.

# Gingerbread Country Church

2 cups shortening
2 cups sugar
2 cups molasses
4 eggs
10 cups all-purpose flour
2 tablespoons ground ginger
2 tablespoons ground cinnamon
2 teaspoons salt
2 teaspoons ground nutmeg
2 teaspoons ground cloves
Patterns on page 77
1/2 cup crushed Jolly Rancher hard candies
Black shoestring licorice
1-1/2 teaspoons water
Red paste food coloring
New paintbrush
ROYAL ICING:
1 package (2 pounds) confectioners' sugar
6 tablespoons meringue powder
12 to 14 tablespoons water
6 tablespoons ground cinnamon
Cardboard cake board (at least 14-inch x 10-inch)
DECORATIONS:
Green and red paste food coloring, corn syrup, ice cream sugar cones, green sprinkles, cornflakes, Rolo candies and flaked coconut

**To make dough:** In a very large bowl, cream shortening and sugar until light and fluffy. Beat in molasses and eggs. Combine the flour, ginger, cinnamon, salt, nutmeg and cloves; gradually add to creamed mixture and mix well. Cover and chill for 2 hours or until easy to handle.

Trace patterns onto waxed paper and cut out. On a lightly floured surface, roll dough in batches to 1/4-in. thickness. Lay patterns on dough and cut out as directed on patterns. Also cut two 12-3/4-in. x 7-1/2-in. rectangles for roof.

Using a sharp knife, score outlines to mark door on front piece where indicated on pattern, being careful not to cut all the way through the dough.

Using a toothpick, draw lines into dough to form shingles on roof pieces. To form siding, press the edge of a ruler into all remaining pieces except the dormers and steeple. (Keep pieces covered to prevent them from drying out.)

With a small knife and ruler, cut two 1/4-in.-wide strips from rolled dough for the cross. Cut two 1/4-in.-wide strips for the door handles. Working freehand, cut a 2-1/2-in.-wide curved pathway. Roll small amounts of dough into balls; press onto pathway, forming stones.

Transfer all dough pieces to parchment paper-lined baking sheets. Bake at 350° for 12-15 minutes or until browned. Cut out the doors completely on the scored lines. Cool gingerbread on pans for 2 minutes before carefully removing to wire racks to cool completely.

Return the front and two side pieces of church to parchment paper-lined baking sheets. Referring to Fig. 1 on page 76, spoon crushed hard candies into the window openings. Bake at 400° for 3-4 minutes or until candy is melted. Working quickly, carefully press licorice pieces onto windows as shown in Fig. 2, creating a leaded glass effect. Cool completely on baking sheets.

Tint water with desired amount of red food coloring. Using new paintbrush, brush mixture over the roof, steeple and dormer pieces; blot gently with paper towels and let dry.

**To make icing:** In a very large bowl, combine confectioners' sugar and meringue powder. Add water; beat on low speed just until combined. Beat on high for 4-5 minutes or until stiff peaks form. Transfer 2 cups icing to another bowl; beat in cinnamon until blended. Keep icing covered at all times with a damp cloth.

**To assemble church:** Pipe cinnamon icing along base and one side of front of church and the adjoining side wall. Place walls at right angles to each other on cake board; prop with small cans to hold in place. Pipe icing along inside and outside edges for added stability. Repeat with second side wall and back of church. Let dry completely.

**For steeple:** Pipe cinnamon icing along one side of front of steeple base and one adjoining side wall. Position at right angles to each other and place on waxed paper; pipe icing along inside edge for added stability. Hold in place until set. Repeat with remaining side and back of steeple base. Repeat for steeple. Let dry completely.

Pipe cinnamon icing along top edges of steeple base; attach steeple. Let dry completely.

**To assemble roof:** Pipe cinnamon icing along top edges of walls. Position roof pieces so there is equal overhang in front and back. Pipe icing along the joining edges. Prop bottoms of roof pieces with cans until roof is completely dry.

Pipe icing onto bottom of steeple and attach to roof. Join the cross pieces with icing; attach to edges of roof.

**For dormers:** On a work surface, position the dormer pieces in pairs so that the pieces are at angles to each other, forming six side dormers and one front dormer. Pipe cinnamon icing along the joining edges. Let dry completely. Pipe icing onto the edges of dormers and attach over windows. Hold in place until secure, about 1 minute.

*(Continued on next page)*

**Finishing touches:** Tint a small amount of icing green and a small amount red. Using a #14 star tip and green icing, pipe wreaths on the doors. Using a #2 round tip and red icing, pipe berries on wreaths. With cinnamon icing, attach handles to doors; attach doors to church front.

For trees, heat a small amount of corn syrup in the microwave until thin; brush over cones. Coat with sprinkles.

For potted shrubs, thin a small amount of icing with water and tint green. Pour over cornflakes; toss to coat. Spread onto waxed paper. Let stand until set. Attach cornflakes to Rolo candies with icing.

Cover cake board with white icing and immediately press pathway into icing. Arrange trees and shrubs around church as desired. Place coconut in a food processor; cover and process until finely chopped. Sprinkle over the church, trees and ground. **Yield:** 1 church.

**Editor's Note:** Meringue powder is available from Wilton Industries. Call 1-800/794-5866 or visit *www.wilton.com*. ✳

## Tips!

### When Making the Gingerbread Country Church:

- Work quickly when placing the licorice on the windows after they come out of the oven—the licorice will stick to the hot, just-melted candy. It's best to cut and bend the licorice pieces ahead of time. Plan a design for your windows and use spice jars or cans to secure your cut licorice pieces until they hold their shape.

- Fun chocolate "pebbles" are available in some specialty candy stores. If you like, let the baked gingerbread pathway cool, then spread it with royal icing and press on the pebbles to make a cobblestone pathway.

- Instead of creating snow by processing shredded coconut in a blender, you could simply sprinkle on powdered sugar. Or, spread white royal icing into a 1/4-inch-thick x 5-inch-long x 3-inch-wide shape, let it harden and grate it with a microplane grater.

- Turn the green "shrubs" into cute potted poinsettias by tinting some of the cornflakes red instead of green. You could also use green cornflakes instead of sprinkles to decorate the cone trees. Simply frost the cones with white royal icing and attach the cornflakes.

**Fig. 1:** Place a piece of the church that has window openings on a parchment paper-lined baking sheet. Use a small spoon to sprinkle crushed candies into the openings.

**Fig. 2:** While the melted candy in the windows is still hot from the oven, use tweezers to position licorice pieces on each window and press the pieces into place.

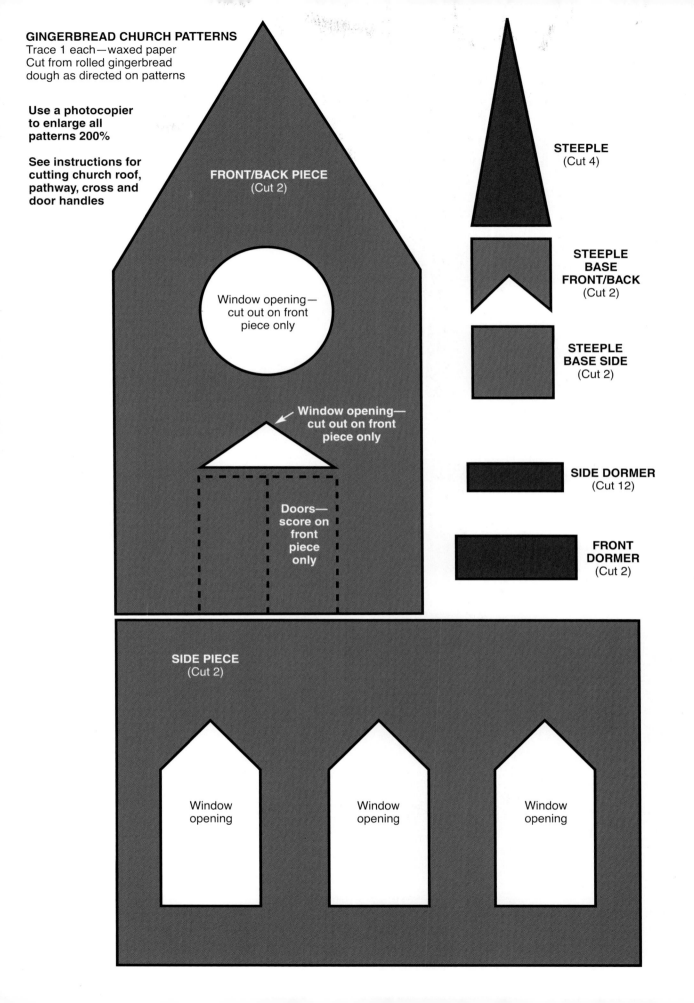

**GINGERBREAD CHURCH PATTERNS**
Trace 1 each—waxed paper
Cut from rolled gingerbread
dough as directed on patterns

**Use a photocopier
to enlarge all
patterns 200%**

**See instructions for
cutting church roof,
pathway, cross and
door handles**

**FRONT/BACK PIECE**
(Cut 2)

Window opening—
cut out on front
piece only

Window opening—
cut out on front
piece only

Doors—
score on
front
piece
only

**STEEPLE**
(Cut 4)

**STEEPLE
BASE
FRONT/BACK**
(Cut 2)

**STEEPLE
BASE SIDE**
(Cut 2)

**SIDE DORMER**
(Cut 12)

**FRONT
DORMER**
(Cut 2)

**SIDE PIECE**
(Cut 2)

Window
opening

Window
opening

Window
opening

# Make Merry by Making Music!

*Host friends for an evening of special appetizers, good company and singing holiday favorites.*

HIT A HIGH NOTE during the holidays by throwing a Christmas party that's all about seasonal music. Your guests are sure to sing your praises!

This tuneful time can take any form you like. Have friends with musical talents? Invite them to bring their instruments—or gather at a home with a piano—and let the musicians perform Yuletide carols for the group. Love karaoke? Set up a machine and invite everyone to take a turn crooning Christmas classics.

In the midst of the merrymaking, treat guests to delicious hot appetizers, plus thirst-quenching drinks and an irresistible dessert to top it all off. You'll find complete recipes starting on this page.

It's an easy way to strike a festive chord and bring friends together in perfect harmony at Christmastime. So go ahead and invite them for some fine-tuned fun—it'll be music to their ears!

## Party Menu

*Chutney-Bacon Cheese Ball*

## Chutney-Bacon Cheese Ball

—*Dena Gurley, Southaven, Mississippi*

1 package (8 ounces) cream cheese, softened
2 cups (8 ounces) shredded sharp cheddar cheese
1 jar (9 ounces) chutney
1 pound bacon strips, chopped
6 green onions, finely chopped
Assorted crackers

**1.** In a large bowl, combine the cheeses. Shape into a ball; top with the chutney. Cover and refrigerate for 8 hours or overnight.

**2.** In a large skillet, cook the bacon over medium heat until crisp. Remove to paper towels; drain. Sprinkle the bacon and onions over the cheese ball. Serve with crackers. **Yield:** 4-1/2 cups.

*Greek Crostini*

# Greek Crostini

*—Mary Shivers, Ada, Oklahoma*

    1 package (8 ounces) cream cheese, softened
   1/4 cup Greek vinaigrette
   1/4 teaspoon dried minced garlic
   1/2 cup Greek pitted olives, chopped
   1/2 cup roasted sweet red peppers, drained
    3 tablespoons butter, softened
   24 slices French bread baguette (1/4 inch thick)
   3/4 cup crumbled goat *or* crumbled feta cheese

In small bowl, combine the cream cheese, vinaigrette and garlic. Stir in olives and red peppers just until blended. Spread butter over baguette slices; place on an ungreased baking sheet. Bake at 400° for 3-4 minutes or until lightly browned. Spread cream cheese mixture over toasts; sprinkle with goat cheese. Bake 2-3 minutes longer or until cheese is softened. **Yield:** 2 dozen.

# Cranberry Brie Wontons

*—Carolyn Cope, Boston, Massachusetts*

1-1/2 cups whole-berry cranberry sauce
    1 teaspoon grated orange peel
   1/2 teaspoon ground nutmeg
    1 pound Brie cheese, rind removed
   72 wonton wrappers
    1 egg, beaten
Oil for deep-fat frying

**1.** In a small bowl, combine the cranberry sauce, orange peel and nutmeg. Place 1 teaspoon cheese and 1 teaspoon cranberry mixture in center of a wonton wrapper. Moisten edges with egg; fold opposite corners together over filling and press to seal. Repeat.

**2.** In an electric skillet, heat 1 in. of oil to 375°. Fry wontons in batches for 30-60 seconds on each side or until golden brown. Drain on paper towels. Serve desired amount immediately. Cool remaining wontons; transfer to freezer containers. Freeze for up to 1 month.

**3.** To use frozen wontons: Place frozen wontons on a greased baking sheet. Bake at 375° for 8-10 minutes or until heated through. **Yield:** 6 dozen.

# Cardamom Cheesecake Bars

*—Judi Oudekerk, Buffalo, Minnesota*

   3/4 cup graham cracker crumbs
    2 tablespoons butter, melted
    2 packages (8 ounces *each*) cream cheese, softened
   1/2 cup sugar
    2 teaspoons ground cardamom, *divided*
    1 teaspoon vanilla extract
    2 eggs, lightly beaten
   1/3 cup all-purpose flour
   1/3 cup quick-cooking oats
   1/3 cup packed brown sugar
   1/4 cup cold butter
   1/3 cup sliced almonds

**1.** In a small bowl, combine graham cracker crumbs and melted butter. Press onto the bottom of a greased 9-in. square baking pan. In large bowl, beat the cream cheese, sugar, 1 teaspoon cardamom and vanilla until smooth. Add eggs; beat on low speed just until combined. Pour over crust.

**2.** In a small bowl, combine the flour, oats, brown sugar and remaining cardamom. Cut in cold butter until crumbly. Stir in almonds. Sprinkle over top.

**3.** Bake at 350° for 35-40 minutes or until center is almost set and topping is golden brown. Cool on a wire rack for 1 hour. Cover and refrigerate for at least 2 hours before serving. Cut into bars. **Yield:** 16 bars.

*Cardamom Cheesecake Bars*

✳ *Special Feature* ✳

*Cran-licious Christmas Punch*
*Hot Apple Pie Drink*

# Hot Apple Pie Drink

—*Country Woman Test Kitchen*

    2 cups unsweetened apple juice
    4 teaspoons brown sugar
    2 teaspoons lemon juice
    1/4 teaspoon ground cinnamon
Dash ground cloves
Dash ground nutmeg
 1-1/2 ounces orange liqueur
 1-1/2 ounces brandy
Sweetened whipped cream and additional ground
    nutmeg, optional

In a small saucepan, heat the first six ingredients until sugar
is dissolved. Remove from the heat; stir in orange liqueur and
brandy. Pour into mugs; garnish with whipped cream and
additional nutmeg if desired. **Yield:** 2 servings.

# Cran-licious Christmas Punch

—*Helen Roland, Miami, Florida*

    2 cups sugar
    2 cups fresh *or* frozen cranberries, thawed
    2 cups water
   10 whole cloves
    2 cinnamon sticks (3 inches)
    2 cups unsweetened pineapple juice
    1 cup lemon juice
    4 cups cold water
    1 liter ginger ale, chilled

**1.** In a Dutch oven, combine the first five ingredients. Cook
over medium heat until the berries pop, about 15 minutes.
Cool slightly.

**2.** Strain mixture through a fine strainer, pressing mixture
with a spoon; discard the pulp and spices. Stir in the juices.
Refrigerate until chilled.

**3.** Just before serving, place mixture in a punch bowl; stir in
water and ginger ale. **Yield:** 18 servings (about 3 quarts).

# Feta-Stuffed
# Prosciutto Mushrooms

—*Karen Moore, Jacksonville, Florida*

        5 whole garlic bulbs
    1/2 cup olive oil, *divided*
        2 fresh rosemary sprigs
    1-1/2 cups crumbled feta cheese
        1 cup crushed garlic-flavored melba rounds
        3 tablespoons lemon juice
    4-1/2 teaspoons minced fresh rosemary
        2 teaspoons grated lemon peel
       12 baby portobello mushrooms
       12 thin slices prosciutto *or* deli ham
        3 tablespoons chicken broth

**1.** Remove papery outer skin from garlic bulbs (do not peel
or separate cloves). Cut top off of each garlic bulb. Brush with
2 tablespoons oil. Top with rosemary sprigs; wrap in heavy-
duty foil. Bake at 425° for 30-35 minutes or until softened.
Cool for 10 minutes.

**2.** Squeeze the softened garlic into a small bowl. Stir in the
cheese, melba crumbs, 1/4 cup olive oil, lemon juice, minced
rosemary and lemon peel.

**3.** Remove the stems from mushrooms (discard or save for
another use). Fold each prosciutto slice in half lengthwise;
wrap around mushrooms and fill with cheese mixture. Place
in a greased 13-in. x 9-in. baking pan; drizzle with remaining
oil. Pour broth around mushrooms.

**4.** Cover and bake at 400° for 20-25 minutes or until heated
through. Uncover; broil 3-4 in. from the heat for 2-3 minutes
or until topping is golden brown. **Yield:** 1 dozen.

# Seasonal
## CRAFTS

*Create your own warmth this Christmas with handmade designs that come from the heart.*

# Keep Tots Cozy In Knit Cardigan

*BUNDLE UP any little one on your Christmas list with this sweet-as-can-be hooded sweater. "I used an Aran pattern, one of my favorites," says Betty Rounds of Bellows Falls, Vermont.*

## MATERIALS NEEDED:

Three 3-ounce skeins of off-white worsted-weight yarn (Betty used Red Heart Super Saver yarn)
Size 8 knitting needles (or size needed to obtain correct gauge)
Cable needle
Stitch holder
Yarn or tapestry needle
Size G/6 (4mm) crochet hook
2-inch x 5-inch piece of cardboard
Measuring tape
Four 1/2-inch brown leather shank buttons
Scissors

**GAUGE:** Working in seed stitch, 8 sts and 14 rows = 2 inches. To save time, take time to check gauge.

**FINISHED SIZE:** Directions are for Toddler size 1 sweater measuring about 24 inches around and 12 inches long from neckline to bottom edge of back of sweater.

## SPECIAL STITCHES:

**SS = seed stitch:**
RS: K 1, p 1 across sts.
WS: K the p sts and p the k sts.

**Cable sts = cable across 6 stitches:**
RS: K 6 sts.
WS: P 6 sts.

Make cable on RS every sixth row as follows: Put the first 3 sts on cable needle, hold sts in front of work, k next 3 sts from needle, then k 3 sts from cable needle.

**Blackberry st = blackberry stitch**
Row 1 (WS): °(K 1, p 1, k 1) into same st, p next 3 sts tog; repeat from ° over number of sts as directed.
Row 2 (RS): P all sts.
Row 3 (WS): P 3 sts tog, (k 1, p 1, k 1) into same st; repeat from ° over number of sts as directed.
Row 4 (RS): P all sts.

**K 1, p 1 rib = knit 1, purl 1 ribbing**
Row 1: K 1, p 1 across row.
Row 2: K the k sts and p the p sts across row.

## DIRECTIONS:

**BACK:** Cast on 52 sts.
Rows 1-3: Work in SS: 52 sts.
Row 4 (WS): Work 5 sts in SS, p 1, k 1, p 6 cable sts, k 1, work Row 1 of blackberry st over next 24 sts, k 1, p 6 for cable sts, k 1, p 1, work 5 sts in SS: 52 sts.
Row 5 (RS): Work 5 sts in SS, k 1, p 1, k 6 cable sts, p 1,

work Row 2 of blackberry st over next 24 sts, p 1, k 6 cable sts, p 1, k 1, work 5 sts in SS: 52 sts.
Row 6 (WS): Work 5 sts in SS, p 1, k 1, p 6 cable sts, k 1, work Row 3 of blackberry st over next 24 sts, k 1, p 6 cable sts, k 1, p 1, work 5 sts in SS: 52 sts.
Row 7 (RS): Work 5 sts in SS, k 1, p 1, k 6 cable sts, p 1, work Row 4 of blackberry st over next 24 sts, p 1, k 6 cable sts, p 1, k 1, work 5 sts in SS: 52 sts.
Repeat Rows 4-7 for seven inches, making cable every sixth row.

**Armholes:** Cast off 2 sts at beginning of each of the next two rows and continue across in established pattern: 48 sts.
Continue in pattern for 4-1/2 inches.
Cast off 7 sts at beginning of next four rows; place remaining 20 sts on stitch holder.

**LEFT FRONT:** Cast on 36 sts.
Rows 1-3: Work in SS: 36 sts.
Row 4 (WS): Work 5 sts in SS, k 1, work Row 1 of blackberry st over next 16 sts, k 1, p 6 cable sts, k 1, p 1, work 5 sts in SS: 36 sts.
Row 5 (RS): Work 5 sts in SS, k 1, p 1, k 6 cable sts, p 1, work Row 2 of blackberry st over next 16 sts, p 1, work 5 sts in SS: 36 sts.
Row 6 (WS): Work 5 sts in SS, k 1, work Row 3 of blackberry st over next 16 sts, k 1, p 6 cable sts, k 1, p 1, work 5 sts in SS: 36 sts.
Row 7 (RS): Work 5 sts in SS, k 1, p 1, k 6 cable sts, p 1, work Row 4 of blackberry st over next 16 sts, p 1, work 5 sts in SS: 36 sts.
Repeat Rows 4-7 for 7 inches, making cable every sixth row.

**Armhole:** Cast off 2 sts at side and continue across in established pattern for 3 more inches: 34 sts.

**Neck shaping:** Shape neck by casting off 6 sts at neck edge over next two neck-edge rows: 22 sts.
Cast off 8 sts at next neck-edge: 14 sts.
When piece measures the same as the back, cast off 7 sts every other side row for shoulder.
Mark button placement evenly spaced down center front.

**RIGHT FRONT:** Cast on 36 sts.
Work buttonholes to correspond with button placement as follows: Work 2 sts in SS on center front edge, cast off 2 sts, continue across row in established pattern. On next row, continue across row in established pattern and cast on 2 sts over cast-off sts in previous row.
Rows 1-3: Work in SS: 36 sts.

*(Continued on next page)*

*(Continued on next page)*

| ABBREVIATIONS | | | |
|---|---|---|---|
| ch(s) | chain(s) | RS | right side |
| inc | increase | sts | stitch(es) |
| k | knit | tog | together |
| p | purl | WS | wrong side |

\* Instructions following asterisk are repeated as directed.

( ) Instructions within parentheses are all worked in the same stitch as directed.

**Row 4 (WS):** Work 5 sts in SS, p 1, k 1, p 6 cable sts, k 1, work Row 1 of blackberry st over next 16 sts, k 1, work 5 sts in SS: 36 sts.

**Row 5 (RS):** Work 5 sts in SS, p 1, work Row 2 of blackberry st over 16 sts, p 1, k 6 cable sts, p 1, k 1, work 5 sts in SS: 36 sts.

**Row 6 (WS):** Work 5 sts in SS, p 1, k1, p 6 cable sts, k 1, work Row 3 of blackberry st over next 16 sts, k 1, work 5 sts in SS: 36 sts.

**Row 7 (RS):** Work 5 sts in SS, p 1, work Row 4 of blackberry st over 16 sts, p 1, k 6 cable sts, p 1, k 1, work 5 sts in SS: 36 sts.

Repeat Rows 4-7 for 7 inches, making cable every sixth row.

**Armhole:** Cast off 2 sts at side and continue across in established pattern for 3 more inches: 34 sts.

**Neck shaping:** Shape neck by casting off 6 sts at neck edge over next two neck-edge rows: 22 sts.

Cast off 8 sts at next neck-edge: 14 sts.

When piece measures the same as the back, cast off 7 sts every other side row for shoulder.

**SLEEVE (make 2):** Cast on 34 sts.

**Rows 1-3:** Work in SS: 34 sts.

**Row 4 (WS):** Work 12 sts in SS, p 1, k 1, p 6 cable sts, k 1, p 1, work 12 sts in SS: 34 sts.

**Row 5 (RS):** Work 12 sts in SS, k 1, p 1, k 6 cable sts, p 1, k 1, work 12 sts in SS: 34 sts.

Repeat Rows 4-5, increasing 1 st at beginning of every sixth row five times and making cable on RS every sixth row: 44 sts.

Work in established pattern without increasing until sleeve measures 7 inches or desired length: 44 sts.

Cast off 3 sts at beginning of every row for 6 rows.

Cast off remaining sts.

**Assembly:** With RS facing, sew shoulder seams together. Then sew sleeves into armholes and underarm seams.

**HOOD: Row 1:** With RS facing, pick up and k 20 sts starting 3 sts in from center front edge, k 20 sts from stitch holder, pick up and k 20 sts along other front edge leaving 3 sts unworked from center edge: 60 sts.

**Rows 2-5:** Work k 1, p 1 rib across: 60 sts.

**Rows 6-7:** Cast on 4 sts at beginning of each row and work k 1, p 1 rib as established across: 68 sts.

**Row 8 (WS):** Work 8 sts in SS, p 1, k 1, p 6 cable sts, k 1, p 1, work Row 1 of blackberry st over next 32 sts, p 1, k 1, 6 cable sts, k 1, p 1, work 8 sts in SS: 68 sts.

**Row 9 (RS):** Work 8 sts in SS, k 1, p 1, k 6 cable sts, p 1, k 1, work Row 2 of blackberry st over next 32 sts, k 1, p 1, k 6 cable sts, p 1, k 1, work 8 sts in SS: 68 sts.

**Row 10 (WS):** Work 8 sts in SS, p 1, k 1, p 6 cable sts, k 1, p 1, work Row 3 of blackberry st over next 32 sts, p 1, k 1, p 6 cable sts, k 1, p 1, work 8 sts in SS: 68 sts.

**Row 11 (RS):** Work 8 sts in SS, k 1, p 1, k 6 cable sts, p 1, k 1, work Row 4 of blackberry st over next 32 sts, k 1, p 1, k 6 cable sts, p 1, k 1, work 8 sts in SS: 68 sts.

Repeat Rows 8-11 for 7 inches, making cable every sixth row.

Cast off all sts, leaving a tail of yarn for seam.

With RS facing, sew bound-off edges together for hood.

Turn 4 cast-on sts along front edge of hood to WS and sew edge to hood to form a channel.

With crochet hook, ch 125 for drawstring. Fasten off, leaving a tail of yarn. Thread string through channel on hood.

**POM-POM (make 2):** For the tie, cut a 10-inch length of yarn. Center tie along the 5-inch length of cardboard piece.

Wrap yarn around tie and width of strip. Each wrap should be smooth but not tight and should lie against the previous wrap. Working back and forth, wrap the length of the strip with five or six layers of yarn.

Carefully bend the cardboard strip lengthwise and remove cardboard without removing the tie.

Knot the ends of the tie with a double knot, pulling the ends tight to make a donut shape.

Without cutting the ends of the tie, cut loops along outermost edge of donut shape. Trim ends so pom-pom measures about 1-1/2 inches across.

Tie a pom-pom to each end of drawstring on hood.

**FINISHING:** Sew buttons to sweater, positioning them opposite the buttonholes. ✳

# Figure on Fun With Wintry Trio

*THREE isn't a crowd when it comes to these cool characters from Lydia Hays of Wichita, Kansas. She designed a cute snowman, penguin and gingerbread man using precut wood shapes.*

**MATERIALS NEEDED (for all):**
Purchased wood pieces—three 3-3/4-inch-tall snowman bodies, four 1-1/4-inch-long mittens, one 1-1/2-inch-high x 1/2-inch-thick heart and two 2-inch-long teardrop shapes
24-inch length of 24-gauge craft wire
Polarfleece—3-1/2-inch x 6-inch piece each of blue and white for hats, 3-1/2-inch square of burgundy for hat and 1-inch x 9-inch piece each of blue, burgundy and white for scarves
Six-strand embroidery floss—burgundy and white
Water container
Paper towels
Foam plate or palette
Acrylic craft paints (Lydia used DecoArt Americana)—Burnt Orange, Burnt Sienna, Camel, Deep Burgundy, Honey Brown, Lamp Black, Light Buttermilk and Terra Cotta
Paintbrushes—small flat, small scruffy brush and liner
Sandpaper
Stylus
Spray sealer
Drill with 1/16-inch bit
Wire cutters
Needle-nose pliers
Fine-line permanent black marker
Ruler
Scissors

**FINISHED SIZE:** Snowman and gingerbread man each measure about 4 inches high x 3 inches wide. Penguin measures about 4-1/2 inches high x 3 inches wide.

**DIRECTIONS:**
**PREPARATION:** Drill a hole through the cuff end of each wooden mitten.

Sand all wood pieces smooth and wipe with a damp paper towel to remove sanding dust.

**PAINTING:** Keep paper towels and a container of water handy to clean brushes. Place small dabs of each paint color onto foam plate or palette as needed. Add coats of paint as needed for complete coverage. Let paint dry after every application. Refer to photo above right as a guide while painting as directed in the instructions that follow.

**Snowman:** Use flat brush to paint a wood snowman Light Buttermilk.

Use flat brush to paint two mittens Deep Burgundy.

Dip flat brush into Deep Burgundy and wipe excess paint onto paper towel. With a nearly dry brush and a circular motion, paint cheeks on snowman's face.

Dip stylus into Lamp Black and add two small dots for eyes. In same way, add three small dots for buttons.

Use flat brush and Burnt Orange to paint carrot nose.
Use marker to outline nose and add mouth.

For snowflakes, use liner and Light Buttermilk to paint a large X on each side of each mitten. In same way, add a horizontal and vertical line through each X. Dip stylus into Light Buttermilk and add a small dot to the end of each line.

Dip stylus into Light Buttermilk and add a tiny dot to each eye and cheek.

**Penguin:** Use flat brush to paint front of a wood snowman Light Buttermilk.

Use flat brush and Lamp Black to paint sides and back of penguin Lamp Black, leaving a curved section of white down the front of penguin.

Use flat brush and Lamp Black to paint each wood teardrop shape.

Dip flat brush into Deep Burgundy and wipe excess paint onto paper towel. With a nearly dry brush and a circular motion, paint cheeks on penguin's face.

Use flat brush and Camel to paint triangle nose on penguin. In same way, paint wood heart.

Dip stylus into Lamp Black and add two small dots for the eyes.

Use marker to outline nose.

Dip stylus into Light Buttermilk and add a tiny dot to each

*(Continued on next page)*

eye and cheek for highlight.

**Gingerbread man:** Use flat brush to paint remaining wood snowman and two mittens Terra Cotta.

Dip flat brush into Deep Burgundy and wipe excess paint onto paper towel. With a nearly dry brush and a circular motion, paint cheeks on gingerbread man's face.

Dip stylus into Lamp Black and add two small dots for eyes.

Dip stylus into Burgundy and add a small dot for nose. In same way, add three small dots for buttons.

Use marker to add mouth.

Use liner and Light Buttermilk to paint a wavy line on each side of each mitten and on each side of face.

Dip stylus into Light Buttermilk and add a tiny dot to each eye and cheek.

**FINISHING:** Following manufacturer's instructions, apply sealer to all wood pieces. Let dry.

**Snowman:** Cut a 12-inch length of craft wire. Thread opposite ends through drilled holes in two burgundy mittens. Twist wire ends to hold. Center wire around neck of snowman and wrap around neck to secure, leaving the ends extending to the front for arms. Wrap each arm around paintbrush handle to coil. Remove brush and shape arms as desired.

Wrap white scarf around neck and tie ends together. Cut 1/8-inch-wide fringe on each end of scarf.

Fold up a short edge of remaining white fleece piece twice, making a 3/8-inch-wide cuff. Glue to hold. Wrap cuff of hat around head and glue to hold. Let dry.

Wrap a 12-inch length of burgundy embroidery floss around hat about 3/4 inch from end. Tie a small bow and trim ends as desired.

**Penguin:** Glue teardrop shapes to opposite sides of penguin for wings. Let dry.

Wrap blue scarf around neck and tie ends together. Cut 1/8-inch-wide fringe on each end of scarf.

Fold up a short edge of remaining blue fleece piece twice, making a 3/8-inch-wide cuff. Glue to hold. Wrap cuff of hat around head and glue to hold. Let dry.

Cut 1/8-inch-wide fringe on end of hat. Wrap a 12-inch length of white embroidery floss around hat about 3/4 inch from end. Tie a small bow and trim ends as desired.

**Gingerbread man:** Thread opposite ends of remaining 12-inch length of craft wire through drilled holes in two terra cotta mittens. Twist wire ends to hold. Center wire around neck of gingerbread man and wrap around neck to secure, leaving the ends extending to the front for arms. Wrap each arm around paintbrush handle to coil. Remove brush and shape arms as desired.

Wrap burgundy scarf around neck and tie ends together. Cut 1/8-inch-wide fringe on each end of scarf.

Fold up a short edge of remaining burgundy fleece piece twice, making a 3/8-inch-wide cuff. Glue to hold. Wrap cuff of hat around head and glue to hold. Let dry.

Wrap a 12-inch length of white embroidery floss around hat about 3/4 inch from end. Tie a small bow and trim ends as desired. ✳

# Toy Soldier Will Salute the Season

*MARCH INTO CHRISTMAS with this holiday cross-stitch. In North Augusta, South Carolina, Ronda Bryce created a standout sentinel that's perfect for framing and displaying.*

**MATERIALS NEEDED:**
Chart on next page
10-inch x 12-inch piece of white 14-count Aida cloth
DMC six-strand embroidery floss in colors listed on color key
Size 24 tapestry needle
Scissors

**FINISHED SIZE:** Toy soldier measures about 6 inches high x 2-1/2 inches wide. Design area is 84 stitches high x 32 stitches wide.

**DIRECTIONS:**
Zigzag or overcast the edges of the Aida cloth to prevent fraying. To find the center of the Aida cloth, fold it in half crosswise, then fold it in half lengthwise and mark where the folds intersect.

Draw lines across the chart, connecting opposite arrows. Mark where the lines intersect. Begin stitching here for a centered design.

Each square on chart represents one set of fabric threads surrounded by four holes. Each stitch is worked over one set of threads with the needle passing through the holes.

The color and/or symbol inside each square on the chart, along with the color key, indicates which color of six-strand embroidery floss to use to make the cross-stitches. Wide lines on chart show where to make the backstitches. See Fig. 1 below for stitch illustrations.

Use 18-inch lengths of floss. Longer strands tend to tangle and fray. Separate the strands of floss and thread the needle with two strands for cross-stitches. Use one strand for backstitches.

To begin stitching, leave a 1-inch tail of floss on back of work and hold tail in place while working the first few stitches over it. To end stitching, run the needle under a few stitches in back before clipping the floss close to work.

When all stitching is complete, and only if necessary, gently wash the stitched piece in lukewarm water. Press right side down on a terry towel to dry.

Frame stitched piece as desired. ✳

**TOY SOLDIER CHART**

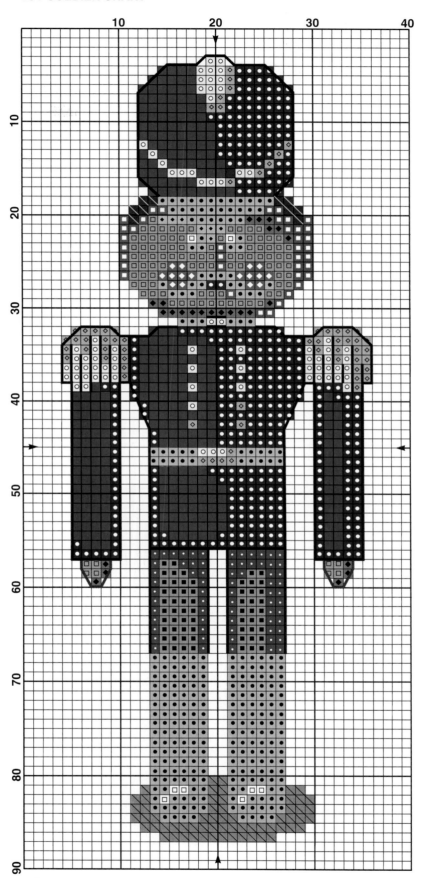

### Fig. 1

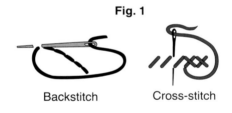

Backstitch          Cross-stitch

| COLOR KEY | DMC |
|---|---|
| ■ Medium Red | 304 |
| ⊡ Black | 310 |
| ◩ Light Steel Gray | 318 |
| ◪ Red | 321 |
| ⊞ Light Brown | 434 |
| ◆ Very Light Brown | 435 |
| ⊡ Tan | 436 |
| ◎ Medium Light Topaz | 725 |
| ◆ Very Light Tan | 738 |
| ◈ Medium Topaz | 783 |
| ■ Dark Delft Blue | 798 |
| ◼ Medium Delft Blue | 799 |
| ◢ Dark Coffee Brown | 801 |
| ◨ Medium Rose | 899 |
| ◻ Winter White | 3865 |
| **BACKSTITCH** | |
| ▬ Black | 310 |
| ▬ Dark Coffee Brown (hands) | 801 |

# Gold Cross Makes A Divine Bookmark

*GET IN THE SPIRIT of the season with this crocheted cross from Janice Fort of Winona, Minnesota. "You could give it as a gift to an avid reader, or even use it as an ornament," she suggests.*

MATERIALS NEEDED:
2-ply gold lamé crochet thread
Size 10 steel crochet hook (or size needed to obtain correct gauge)
3-inch square of lightweight cardboard
Yarn or tapestry needle
Scissors

GAUGE: At the end of Round 3, piece measures about 1-1/2 inches wide. A slight variation in gauge will change the finished size a bit.

FINISHED SIZE: Bookmark measures about 8-1/2 inches high x 3-1/2 inches wide.

DIRECTIONS:
CROSS: Round 1: Ch 4, join in first ch made to form a ring.

Round 2: Ch 3 for first dc, dc in ring, ch 2, [work 2 dcs in ring, ch 2] three times, join with a sl st in top of beginning ch-3: 8 dcs and 4 ch-2 sps. Leave beginning thread hang in back to mark back.

Round 3: Sl st to next ch-2 sp, (ch 3 for first dc, dc, ch 3, 2 dcs) in same sp, ch 1, ° (work 2 dcs, ch 3, 2 dcs) in next ch-2 sp, ch 1; repeat from ° around, join with a sl st in top of

beginning ch-3, turn: 16 dcs and 8 ch-sps.

First point: Row 1: Ch 4 for first dc and ch-1 sp, (work 3 dcs, ch 3, 3 dcs) in next ch-sp, ch 1, sk next 2 dcs, dc in next ch-sp: 8 dcs and 3 ch-sps.

Row 2: Ch 4 for first dc and ch-1 sp, turn, (work 4 dcs, ch 4, 4 dcs) in next ch-3 sp, ch 1, sk next 3 dcs and first ch in next ch-sp, dc in next ch: 10 dcs and 3 sps.

Row 3: Ch 4 for first dc and ch-1 sp, turn, (work 5 dcs, ch 5, 5 dcs) in next ch-4 sp, ch 1, sk next 4 dcs and first ch in next ch-sp, dc in next ch: 12 dcs and 3 sps. Fasten off.

Second and third points: With sl knot on hk, join thread in same sp as last dc of first point Row 1.

Row 1: Ch 4 for first dc and ch-1 sp, (work 3 dcs, ch 3, 3 dcs) in next ch-sp, ch 1, sk next 2 dcs, dc in next ch-sp: 8 dcs and 3 sps.

Rows 2-3: Repeat Rows 2-3 of first point.

Long point: With sl knot on hk, join thread in first remaining ch-sp of Round 3.

Rows 1-3: Repeat Rows 1-3 of first point.

Row 4: Ch 4 for first dc and ch-1 sp, turn, work (6 dcs, ch 6, 6 dcs) in next ch-5 sp, ch 1, sk next 5 dcs and first ch in next ch-sp, dc in next ch, turn: 14 dcs and 3 sps.

Row 5: Ch 4 for first dc and ch-1 sp, turn, work (7 dcs, ch 3, 7 dcs) in next ch-6 sp, ch 1, sk next 6 dcs and first ch in next ch-sp, dc in next ch: 16 dcs and 3 sps.

Edging: Sc in first ch-sp along edge, ch 3, sl st in first ch made (picot made), sc in same sp, [(sc, ch 3-picot, sc) in next sp] four more times along long point, ° work three sc in next sp, [(sc, ch 3-picot, sc) in next sp] three times, sc in next 5 dcs, (sc, ch 3-picot, sc) in ch-sp on end of point, sc in next 5 dcs, [(sc, ch 3-picot, sc) in next sp] three times; repeat from ° two more times, work 3 scs in next sp, [(sc, ch 3-picot, sc) in next sp] five times along long point, sc in next 7 dcs, (sc, ch 3-picot, sc) in ch-sp, sc in next 7 dcs, (sc, ch 3-picot, sc) in next ch-sp, join with a sl st in beginning sc. Fasten off.

Use yarn or tapestry needle to weave in all loose ends.
TASSEL: Wind thread 25 times around cardboard.

Cut a 6-inch length of thread. Slip one end of thread under loops on top edge of cardboard. Pull ends to gather thread together tightly. Tie ends in a knot.

Bend cardboard and carefully slip thread off cardboard. Cut another 6-inch length of thread. Wrap thread around tassel about 1/4 inch from top. Knot ends and trim close to knot. Cut opposite ends to form fringe.

Tie tassel to long point of cross. Trim ends close to knot. ✳

```
                   ABBREVIATIONS
  ch(s)    chain(s)              sl    slip
  dc(s)    double crochet(s)     sl st  slip stitch
   hk      hook                  sp    space(s)
  sc(s)    single crochet(s)     st(s)  stitch(es)
   sk      skip

     ( ) Instructions within parentheses are all
         worked in the same space as directed.

    * [ ] Instructions following asterisk or between
          brackets are repeated as directed.
```

# Send Warm Wishes With Frosty Fellow

*YOU'LL MELT HEARTS during the Christmas season when you give friends and family this cute snowman card. The design comes from Sandy Rollinger of Apollo, Pennsylvania.*

## MATERIALS NEEDED:

Patterns on this page
Tracing paper and pencil
5-inch x 7-inch white card
Card stock—one sheet or scraps each of aqua, green, light blue, orange and white
One sheet or scrap of coordinating print scrapbook paper
Paper crimper
1/2-inch sun paper punch (optional)
Blue medium-point marker or computer with printer (for printing word)
Black permanent fine-line marker
Clear seed beads (for snow)
Seven black seed beads
Two green doll buttons
Toothpick
Craft glue for paper
Ruler
Scissors

**FINISHED SIZE:** Card is 7 inches high x 5 inches wide.

## DIRECTIONS:

Refer to photo above as a guide while assembling card as directed in the instructions that follow.

Cut a 5-inch x 7-inch rectangle of print paper. With fold of card at the left, glue the paper piece to front of card.

Cut a 3-1/2-inch x 4-inch rectangle of aqua card stock. Use scissors to make a slight inward curve on each side of the rectangle. Glue piece at an angle to front of card.

Trace snowman, nose and hat patterns onto tracing paper with pencil. Cut out shapes following outline of patterns. Cut shapes from card stock as directed on patterns.

Referring to photo for direction of ridges in the crimping, run the snowman, hat top, hat brim and nose pieces through paper crimper.

Glue snowman, nose and hat shapes to front of card.

Apply a thin bead of glue around the outside edges of the aqua paper and sprinkle clear beads over the glue while it is still wet, using toothpick to help place beads. In the same way, add glue and beads to the top edge of nose.

Glue on two black beads for the eyes and five black beads for the mouth.

Glue two buttons to front of snowman.

Punch or cut a sun shape from print paper. Glue sun shape below nose. Use black marker to draw a straight vertical line from tip of nose to top of sun shape and add a small bow at the top.

Use computer or blue marker to print "CELEBRATE" on white card stock. Trim card stock to a 1-3/4-inch x 2-inch rectangle.

Glue word piece to a piece of light blue card stock. Trim light blue card stock, leaving a 1/4-inch margin on all sides.

Glue assembled piece to front of card. Let dry. ✳

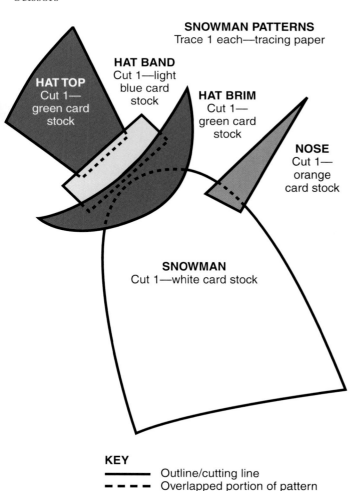

**SNOWMAN PATTERNS**
Trace 1 each—tracing paper

**HAT TOP**
Cut 1—green card stock

**HAT BAND**
Cut 1—light blue card stock

**HAT BRIM**
Cut 1—green card stock

**NOSE**
Cut 1—orange card stock

**SNOWMAN**
Cut 1—white card stock

**KEY**
——— Outline/cutting line
- - - - Overlapped portion of pattern

# Add Dazzle with Metallic Necklace

*TO FASHION a festive look anytime, finish off an outfit with this three-strand stunner made by Sarah Farley of Menomonee Falls, Wisconsin. It adds a dress-up look all year long.*

**MATERIALS NEEDED:**
.014-inch-diameter beading wire (Sarah used Satin Silver Soft Flex)—two 26-inch lengths, two 23-inch lengths and two 20-inch lengths
One hundred-two 2mm 14K gold-filled crimp beads
Pair of three-loop gold-tone chandeliers
52 bronze Toho 8/0 seed beads
Eight 30mm flat oval bronze beads
Eighteen 10mm gold-and-brown multicolored foil beads
Eight 4mm light Colorado topaz faceted crystal beads
Seven 6mm brown plastic diamond faceted beads
Seven 6mm gold plastic diamond faceted beads
Gold-tone lobster claw clasp with jump ring
4.5mm 14K gold-filled split ring
5-inch length of 14K gold-filled open-loop chain
Crimper
Ruler
Wire cutters

**FINISHED SIZE:** Necklace measures about 27 to 32 inches long.

**DIRECTIONS:**

**OUTER STRAND:** Thread both 26-inch lengths of wire through a crimp bead and through the outer loop of one chandelier. Thread ends of wires back through crimp bead and pull to close loop. Crimp close to chandelier. Trim excess wire close to crimp bead.

° Thread both wire strands through a crimp bead, seed bead, flat bronze bead, another seed bead and crimp bead. Separate the wires. On one wire, thread a crimp bead, seed bead, foil bead, seed bead and crimp bead. On other wire, thread a crimp bead, 4mm topaz bead, two crimp beads, a 4mm topaz bead and crimp bead.

Repeat from ° three more times.

Thread both wires through a crimp bead, seed bead, flat bronze bead, seed bead and two crimp beads. Thread both wires through the outer loop of the second chandelier. Thread ends of both wires back through the last crimp bead and pull to close loop, creating a 24-inch-long outer strand of necklace. Crimp close to second chandelier. Trim excess wire close to crimp bead.

Center the third flat bronze bead on the beaded strand. Push the adjacent seed beads up against the flat bronze bead and push the adjacent crimp beads up against the seed beads. Crimp the crimp beads.

Position the end of the next flat bronze bead so that it is 4 inches from the end of the center flat bronze bead. Push the adjacent seed beads up against the flat bronze bead and use crimp beads to hold them in place as before.

Secure remaining flat bronze beads in the same way, continuing to position them 4 inches apart.

On one wire, center a foil bead and the adjacent seed beads between two flat bronze beads and use crimp beads to hold them in place as before. Secure remaining foil beads in the same way.

Between two flat bronze beads on the other wire, position the two topaz beads so that each is about 1 inch from the closest flat bronze bead and use crimp beads to hold them in place. Secure remaining topaz beads in the same way.

**CENTER STRAND:** Thread both 23-inch lengths of wire through a crimp bead and through the center loop of one chandelier. Thread ends of wires back through crimp bead and pull to close loop. Crimp close to chandelier. Trim excess wire close to crimp bead.

° Separate wires. On one wire, thread a crimp bead, 6mm brown bead and crimp bead. On other wire, thread a crimp bead, 6mm gold bead and crimp bead. Bring wires together and thread both though a crimp bead, seed bead, foil bead, seed bead and crimp bead.

Repeat from ° five more times.

Separate wires. On one wire, thread a crimp bead, 6mm brown bead and crimp bead. On the other wire, thread a crimp bead, 6mm gold bead and two crimp beads. Thread both ends of wire through center loop of second chandelier and back through the last crimp bead. Pull to close loop, creating a 22-inch-long center strand. Crimp close to chandelier. Trim excess wire close to crimp bead.

Find the center of beaded strand. Position a 6mm brown

bead about 1/2 inch from center point and position a 6mm gold bead about 1/2 inch from center point on other side. Use crimp beads to hold them in place.

Position the two foil beads on opposite sides of center point so that they are an equal distance from center point and measure about 3 inches apart. Push adjacent seed beads up against foil beads and use crimp beads to hold them in place.

Secure remaining foil beads in the same way, continuing to position them about 3 inches apart.

Position the 6mm brown and 6mm gold beads evenly spaced between the foil beads and use crimp beads to hold them in place.

INNER STRAND: Thread both 20-inch lengths of wire through a crimp bead and through inner loop of one chandelier. Thread ends of wires back through crimp bead and pull to close loop. Crimp close to chandelier. Trim excess wire close to crimp bead.

° Separate wires. On one wire, thread a crimp bead, seed bead, foil bead, seed bead and crimp bead. Repeat on other wire. Bring wires together and thread a crimp bead, seed bead, flat bronze bead, seed bead and crimp bead.

Repeat from ° two more times.

Separate wires. On one wire, thread a crimp bead, seed bead, foil bead, seed bead and crimp bead. On other wire, thread a crimp bead, seed bead, foil bead, seed bead and two crimp beads. Thread both ends of wire through inner loop of second chandelier and back through the last crimp bead. Pull to close loop, creating a 22-inch-long inner strand. Crimp close to chandelier. Trim excess wire close to crimp bead.

Center second flat bronze bead on wire. Push adjacent seed beads up against flat bronze bead and use crimp beads to hold them in place. Position the remaining flat bronze beads 3-1/2 inches from the ends of the center flat bronze bead and secure the same as before.

Position foil beads so that all foil beads and flat bronze beads are spaced about 1 inch apart along strand. Push adjacent seed beads up against foil beads and use crimp beads to hold them in place.

FINISHING: Use the jump ring to attach the lobster claw clasp to the end of one chandelier. Use the 4.5mm split ring to attach the 5-inch length of open-loop chain to the other chandelier. ✳

---

# Chunky Bracelet Is Big on Style

*CINCHING a silver chain creates the base of this eye-catching accent. "Then I attached blue beads for a bit of color," says Sarah Farley of Menomonee Falls, Wisconsin.*

MATERIALS NEEDED:
12-inch length of beading wire (or desired length of bracelet plus four inches)
Beading needle
78-inch length of small open-loop silver chain
24 silver head pins
Twenty-four 6mm beads (Sarah used a combination of clear, frosted, light blue and ice blue beads)
Two silver clam clasps
Silver toggle clasp with jump rings
Round-nose pliers
Chain-nose pliers
Wire cutters
G-S Hypo cement or jewelry glue

FINISHED SIZE: Bracelet measures about 8 inches long x 3/4 inch wide.

DIRECTIONS:
Thread needle with beading wire and tie the wire ends in a knot close to the end. Use wire cutters to trim excess wire close to knot.

Thread the unknotted end of beading wire through the hole in one end of a clam shell until the knot rests inside the shell. Add a drop of glue to secure. When dry, use chain-nose pliers to close and secure clam clasp.

Thread the needle through every other loop on the silver chain, drawing up the loops close to each other.

Thread remaining clam clasp onto wire. Tie a knot as close as possible to the chain, making bracelet about 7 inches long or desired length. Add a drop of glue to secure. When dry, use chain-nose pliers to close and secure clam clasp.

Insert a head pin in a bead. Attach bead to chain where desired, using round-nose pliers to make a loop close to the top of the bead. Trim excess. Repeat to add remaining beads.

Attach the toggle clasps to the clam clasps at the opposite ends of bracelet. ✳

## Stitched Santa Suits Christmas Trees

*THIS JOLLY ELF ORNAMENT from Renee Dent of Conrad, Montana delivers extra holiday cheer. "For added dimension, I accented the cross-stitching with beads," Renee says.*

### MATERIALS NEEDED:

Chart on this page
5-inch square of white 14-count Aida cloth
3-1/2-inch x 4-3/4-inch piece of red felt
DMC six-strand embroidery floss in colors listed on color key
Size 24 tapestry needle
Sixty-seven white glass seed beads
Beading needle
8-inch length of 1/4-inch-wide red satin ribbon
Polyester stuffing
All-purpose white thread
Standard sewing supplies

**Fig. 1**

Cross-stitch

Backstitch

| COLOR KEY | DMC |
|---|---|
| ☐ White | |
| ◼ Medium Red. . . . . . . . . . . . . . . . . | 304 |
| ◪ Peach . . . . . . . . . . . . . . . . . . . . | 353 |
| ☐ Cream . . . . . . . . . . . . . . . . . . . | 712 |
| ◼ Royal Blue . . . . . . . . . . . . . . . . | 797 |
| ☒ Light Tawny . . . . . . . . . . . . . . . | 951 |
| **BACKSTITCH** | |
| — Dark Hunter Green. . . . . . . . . | 3345 |
| — Black Brown. . . . . . . . . . . . . . | 3371 |
| **HALF CROSS-STITCH** | |
| ╱ White (on eyes) | |
| • = Bead placement | |

**FINISHED SIZE**: Excluding hanging loop, ornament measures about 3-3/4 inches high x 2-3/4 inches wide. Design area is 48 stitches high x 31 stitches wide.

### DIRECTIONS:

Zigzag or overcast the edges of the Aida cloth to prevent fraying. To find the center of the Aida cloth, fold it in half crosswise, then fold it in half lengthwise and mark where the folds intersect.

Draw lines across the chart, connecting opposite arrows. Mark where lines intersect. Begin stitching here for a centered design.

Each square on chart represents one set of fabric threads surrounded by four holes. Each stitch is worked over one set of threads with the needle passing through the holes.

The color and/or symbol inside each square on the chart, along with the color key, indicates which color of six-strand embroidery floss to use to make cross-stitches. Wide lines on the chart show where to make backstitches. See Fig. 1 below left for stitch illustrations.

Use 18-inch lengths of floss. Longer strands tend to tangle and fray. Separate the strands of floss and thread the needle with two strands for all cross-stitches and half cross-stitches. Use one strand for backstitches. Use one strand of white floss to sew on beads.

To begin stitching, leave a 1-inch tail of floss on back of work and hold tail in place while working the first few stitch-

**SANTA CHART**

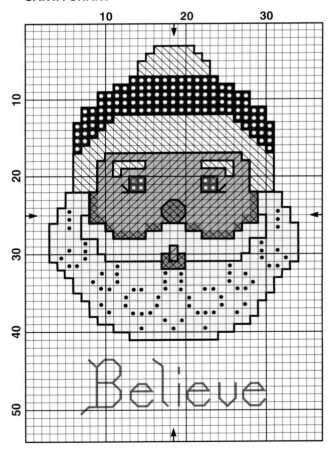

es over it. To end stitching, run the needle under a few stitches in back before clipping the floss close to work.

When all stitching is complete, sew on beads where shown on chart.

FINISHING: With design centered, trim stitched piece to a 4-3/4-inch-high x 3-1/2-inch-wide rectangle.

With right sides together and edges matching, pin stitched piece to felt piece.

Sew around outside edges with a 1/4-inch seam, leaving an opening for turning along the bottom.

Clip corners diagonally and turn ornament inside out. Stuff ornament firmly.

Turn raw edges of opening in and hand-sew closed.

Make an overhand knot 1 inch from each end of the ribbon piece. Hand-sew knots to opposite top corners of ornament for hanger. ✳

# Top Hat Snowman Is a Dapper Accent

*DRESS UP any nook or cranny for the winter season with this frosty figure. "It's easy to make using a purchased hat and wood snowman," says Irene Wegener of Corning, New York.*

## MATERIALS NEEDED:
3-3/8-inch-diameter black felt top hat
2-7/8-inch-high split wood snowman
Water container
Paper towels
Foam plate or palette
Acrylic craft paints—black, blush, dark blue, dark red, gold, orange and white
Paintbrushes—small flat, 1/4-inch angle and liner
Toothpick
Matte sealer
1-inch x 6-inch strip of plaid fabric
White heavy thread or crochet cotton
Hand-sewing needle
Spanish moss
Artificial pine boughs
Artificial red pip berry sprigs
Glue gun and glue sticks
Scissors

FINISHED SIZE: Top hat snowman measures about 4-1/2 inches high x 4 inches wide.

## DIRECTIONS:
PAINTING: Keep paper towels and a container of water handy to clean brushes. Place small dabs of each paint color onto foam plate or palette as needed. Add coats of paint as needed for complete coverage. Let paint dry after every application unless instructions say otherwise. Refer to photo at right as a guide while painting as directed in the instructions that follow.

Use flat brush and white to basecoat entire wood snowman except hat.

Use flat brush and black to paint wood hat.

Use flat brush and dark red to paint snowman's vest. See Fig. 1 above right.

Use angle brush and black to shade outer edge of vest.

Dip the end of a paintbrush handle into black and add three buttons to center front of vest. In same way, add two small dots for eyes and five smaller dots for mouth.

Dip the toothpick into gold and add two tiny dots to each

black button for the buttonholes.

Dip flat brush into dark blue and wipe excess paint off on paper towel. With a nearly dry brush, shade the outer edge of face and the body below vest.

Dip flat brush into dark red and wipe excess paint off on paper towel. With a nearly dry brush, use a circular motion to add cheeks.

Apply matte sealer to snowman following manufacturer's instructions.

HAT: Thread hand-sewing needle with heavy white thread or crochet cotton. Referring to the photo for position, stitch three snowflakes on front of hat.

FINISHING: Glue Spanish moss, artificial greens and pip berry sprigs inside hat, leaving room in the center for the snowman.

Tie strip of plaid fabric around snowman's neck for scarf and glue as needed to hold.

Glue snowman inside center of hat. Let dry. ✳

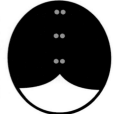

Fig. 1
Painting vest

# 'Paws' to Make a Polar Bear Frame

*ANY CUBBYHOLE in your home will be brighter with Sandy Rollinger's whimsical photo holder. In Apollo, Pennsylvania, she decorated a purchased frame using stamps, paint and clay.*

**MATERIALS NEEDED:**
Unfinished wood pieces—8-inch square picture frame, two 2-inch snowflakes and one 2-1/2-inch snowflake
Water container
Paper towels
Foam plate or palette
Acrylic craft paints (Sandy used FolkArt)—Jamaican Sea, Licorice, Pearl White Metallic, Periwinkle, Pink and Winter White
Paintbrushes—medium flat and small round
Small piece of household sponge
White oven-bake clay (Sandy used Sculpey Ultra-Light White)
1/2-inch-high letter stamps
Clay knife or craft knife
Clay oven and foil-lined baking tray
Two 1/4-inch wiggle eyes
Scrubby pad
Toothpicks
Craft glue
Ruler

**FINISHED SIZE:** Frame measures about 9 inches high x 9 inches wide.

**DIRECTIONS:**
Refer to the photo above as a guide while painting and assembling frame as directed in the instructions that follow.

**CLAY PIECES:** Condition the clay.

**Letters:** Roll 11 dime-size balls of clay for the snowball letters. Roll the balls over the scrubby pad to add texture. Use letter stamps to press one letter into each ball to spell "JUST CHILLIN." Place letters on foil-lined baking tray.

**Head:** Roll and flatten clay to make a 2-inch x 2-1/2-inch oval for polar bear's head. Roll and flatten two dime-size balls of clay for ears. Use scrubby pad to add texture to head and ears. Press ears to back of polar bear's head.

Use toothpick to add smile, muzzle line and three dots on each side of muzzle.

Roll a 5/8-inch flattened oval for nose.

Place pieces on foil-lined baking tray.

**Scarf:** Roll and slightly flatten a 2-inch oval of clay for base.

Roll a 1/4-inch-thick rectangle of clay. Use clay or craft knife to cut two 3/4-inch-wide x 2-inch-long pieces for scarf ends. Cut slits in one end of each piece for fringe.

Press one scarf end to the back of scarf base and press the other to the front of scarf base.

**Paws:** Roll two large marble-size pieces of clay for paws. Use scrubby pad to add texture to each. Use toothpick to mark two lines on each paw.

Gently press each paw onto the frame's edge where they will be attached later, making an indentation on the back of each. Remove paws from frame and place them on foil-lined baking tray.

Bake all clay pieces following manufacturer's instructions. Let cool.

**PAINTING:** Keep paper towels and a container of water handy to clean brushes. Place small dabs of each paint color onto foam plate or palette as needed. Add coats of paint as needed for complete coverage. Let paint dry after every application.

**Frame:** Dip sponge piece into Winter White and use an up-and-down motion to sponge-paint entire frame.

Pour a small amount of Jamaican Sea onto foam plate or palette. Mix in a small amount of Winter White and blend to make light blue. Sponge-paint light blue on front of frame the same as before, allowing some white paint to show through.

In the same way, sponge-paint inside edge of frame with Jamaican Sea and outside edge of frame with Periwinkle.

**Clay pieces:** Paint each snowball letter Pearl White.

Use round brush to paint each indented letter Periwinkle.

Use flat brush and Periwinkle to shade outer edges of polar bear's face, ears and paws.

Use round brush and Pink to paint inside of each ear.

Use round brush and Licorice to paint nose, eyebrows, muzzle line, muzzle dots and mouth.

Use flat brush and Jamaican Sea to paint scarf.

Dip end of paintbrush handle into Periwinkle and add dots to scarf.

Use round brush and Pearl White to add highlight to nose.

Use flat brush and Pearl White to paint each snowflake.

Mix a bit of Jamaican Sea with Pearl White and use to highlight head, paws and each snowflake.

**FINISHING:** Glue snowflakes, letters and scarf to frame. Glue nose and wiggle eyes to polar bear's head.

Glue head to scarf and glue paws to edges of frame where planned.

Let frame dry at least two hours before inserting photo. ✷

# *Punch a Flurry of Paper Snowflakes*

*YOU'LL FALL INTO FUN with these frosty tree ornaments from Loretta Mateik of Petaluma, California. The glittery snowflakes could also make festive trims for Christmas gift boxes and bags.*

**MATERIALS NEEDED** (for one):
Sheet or scraps of white card stock
2-inch snowflake punch
Spray adhesive
Newspaper
Fine glitter—iridescent or white and light blue
Two round blue paper brads
1/8-inch circle punch
8-inch length of heavy thread or ribbon for hanging
Craft glue

**FINISHED SIZE:** Excluding hanging loop, each snowflake ornament measures about 2 inches high x 2 inches wide.

**DIRECTIONS:**
Use snowflake punch to punch five snowflakes from white card stock.

Use 1/8-inch circle punch to punch a hole through the center of each snowflake.

Place snowflakes on newspaper-covered surface. Spray snowflakes with adhesive following manufacturer's instructions. While still wet, sprinkle iridescent or white and light blue glitter on snowflakes. Let dry. Tap off excess glitter.

Turn snowflakes over and apply glitter to the back of each snowflake in the same way.

Stack three snowflakes with edges even and insert a brad through the punched holes. Spread ends of brad flat to hold it in place. Bend the ends of the top snowflakes forward to create dimension.

Stack the two remaining snowflakes and attach a brad the same as before.

With wrong sides together, glue the centers of the two assembled snowflake pieces together. Let dry.

Use 1/8-inch circle punch to make a hole through one end of snowflake. Insert thread or ribbon through hole and tie ends together to form hanging loop. ✷

# Two-Piece Skirt
# Is Twice As Nice

*AT THE ROOT of this elegant design by CW Craft Editor Jane Craig is the green bottom piece. The tree stand rests on top of it and is hidden by a separate red piece draped over the stand.*

**MATERIALS NEEDED:**
58-inch-wide woven crushed velvet—1-1/2 yards each of green and red
3 yards of 44-inch-wide coordinating fabric for lining
All-purpose thread to match fabrics
7-1/4 yards of gold metallic braid trim
Three hook and eye sets
Quilter's marking pen or pencil
Standard sewing supplies

**FINISHED SIZE:** Bottom skirt measures about 52 inches across. Top skirt measures about 26 inches across.

**DIRECTIONS:**
**BOTTOM TREE SKIRT:** From green velvet, cut a 49-1/2-inch circle. See Fig. 1 below right.

From red velvet, cut a 52-1/2-inch circle using same technique as before. Then cut 3-1/2 inches from the outer edge of circle to make a 3-1/2-inch-wide red band.

Sew the red band to the outer edge of the green circle with a 1/4-inch seam.

From lining fabric, cut two 1-1/2-yard lengths. Sew long edges together with a 1/2-inch seam to make a piece that measures about 54 inches x 87 inches.

With right sides together, pin bottom tree skirt to lining fabric. Cut along edge of bottom tree skirt to trim excess lining fabric. Sew lining and bottom tree skirt together with a

1/4-inch seam, leaving an opening for turning. Turn tree skirt right side out. Turn raw edges in and hand-sew closed.

Pin braid on right side of bottom tree skirt, covering seam between green and red areas. Sew braid in place.

**TOP TREE SKIRT:** Using same technique as before, cut a 26-1/2-inch circle each from red velvet and lining fabric.

With right sides facing, pin red top tree skirt to lining.

Use quilter's marking pen or pencil to draw a circle on the center of top tree skirt to accommodate the trunk of your tree. Draw a straight line from the edge of center circle to the outside edge of top tree skirt for the opening.

Referring to Fig. 2 below right, sew lining and top tree skirt together around outside edge with a 1/4-inch seam. Stitch around marked center circle line. Stitch a straight line 1/4 inch from marked straight line on each side, leaving an opening for turning along one straight line. Clip into seams so seams lie flat. Turn tree skirt right side out. Turn raw edges of opening in and hand-sew opening closed.

Sew braid to outer edge of top tree skirt. Hand-sew hook and eye sets evenly spaced along each edge of opening. ✳

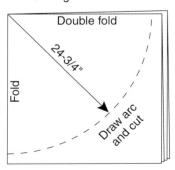

**Fig. 1**
Cutting bottom circle

Double fold

Fold

24-3/4"

Draw arc and cut

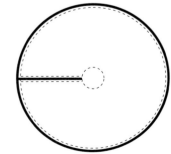

**Fig. 2**
Sewing lining and top tree skirt together

# Felted Handbag Will Welcome Winter

*SHOW YOUR STYLE at Christmas and year-round by knitting this bold striped purse. "I love to give handmade bags like this as gifts," says Mary Baker of Glen Cove, New York.*

**MATERIALS NEEDED:**
Worsted-weight wool yarn—two skeins each of red and black (Mary used Patons Bright Red Classic 100% Wool yarn and Patons Black Classic 100% Wool yarn)
One skein of black mohair novelty yarn (Mary used Patons Moonlight Mohair Black)
24-inch-long size 13 circular needle
Four stitch markers
Magnetic purse closure
Two 2-inch squares of black felt
Yarn or tapestry needle
Needle-nose pliers
Two pillowcases or laundry bags
Rubber band
Four spring-type clothespins
Plastic shopping bags
Two towels
Scissors

**FINISHED SIZE:** Excluding the straps, purse measures about 12 inches wide x 8 inches deep x 7-1/2 inches high. Finished size may vary depending on felting.

**DIRECTIONS:**
**KNITTING:** Purse is made using two strands of black, two strands of red and three strands of novelty yarn throughout.

    **Bottom:** With black, cast on 28 sts.
    **Rows 1-28:** K each row: 28 sts.
    Bind off.
    **Body: Round 1:** With red, pick up 28 sts along one edge of bottom piece, place stitch marker, pick up 28 sts along adjoining edge, place marker, pick up 28 sts, place marker, pick up 28 sts, place marker: 112 sts.
    **Rounds 2-11:** K around: 112 sts.
    **Round 12:** With black, k around: 112 sts.
    **Rounds 13-14:** With novelty yarn, p around: 112 sts.
    **Round 15:** With black, k around: 112 sts.
    **Rounds 16-25:** With red, k around: 112 sts.
    **Rounds 26-29:** Repeat Rounds 12-15: 112 sts.
    **Rounds 30-39:** With red, k around: 112 sts.
    **Rounds 40-43:** Repeat Rounds 12-15: 112 sts.
    **Rounds 44-49:** With red, k around: 112 sts.
    **Round 50:** With black, k around: 112 sts.
    **Round 51:** With novelty yarn, p around: 112 sts.
    **Rounds 52-57:** Repeat Rounds 50 and 51: 112 sts.
    With black, bind off knitwise.
    Use yarn or tapestry needle to weave in all loose ends.
    **I-cord strap (make two):** With red, cast on 4 sts.
    K across, do not turn. Slide sts to opposite end of needle, k across. Repeat until cord measures about 28 inches.
    Weave in loose ends.

**FELTING:** Place purse in a pillowcase or laundry bag and close. Place straps in a separate pillowcase or laundry bag and close. Keep the straps separated by placing a rubber band around the center of the pillowcase or laundry bag.

    Place items in washing machine and set washer for a small load. Add a bath towel and 1/4 cup of Palmolive Liquid detergent without grease cutter. Wash with hot water for 15 minutes. Remove items and rinse them. Squeeze out excess water. Do not put in dryer.

**ATTACHING STRAPS:** Referring to Fig. 1 below, use knitting needle to make holes through top of purse.

    Using needle-nose pliers, pull strap ends through the holes from the outside of purse through the holes on the sides of purse. Repeat on opposite side of purse. Tie straps in a knot at the sides of purse.

**DRYING:** Place purse on a dry towel on a protected surface. Shape purse and fill with scrunched-up plastic bags to maintain desired shape. Tuck in sides and hold each side with two clothespins.

**FINISHING:** Attach each side of magnetic closure to the center of a felt piece.

    With black yarn, hand-sew felt pieces centered along inside top edges of purse. ✳

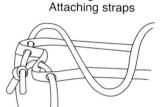

**Fig. 1**
Attaching straps

**ABBREVIATIONS**
k  knit
p  purl
sts  stitch(es)

Paper towels
Foam plate or palette
Acrylic craft paints—black, blush, flesh, gold and white
Small flat paintbrush
Toothpick
Black fine-line marker
White textured doll hair or white yarn
Ruler
Glue gun and glue stick
Scissors
Standard sewing supplies

**FINISHED SIZE:** Napkin holder shown measures 14 inches high x 5-1/2 inches wide.

**EDITOR'S NOTE:** Depending on the size of your potato masher handle, the opening of the hat may need to be made larger or smaller. Also, the beard may need to be made longer or shorter.

**DIRECTIONS:**
Measure 2-1/4 inches down from the end of potato masher handle and drill an 1/8-inch-deep hole into handle for nose.

Drill a hole through the top of the handle if it does not have one. Sand handle.

Glue domed furniture plug into hole for nose. Let dry.

**PAINTING:** Keep paper towels and a container of water handy to clean brush. Place small dabs of each paint color onto foam plate or palette as needed. Add coats of paint as needed for complete coverage. Let paint dry after every application. Refer to photo at left as a guide while painting as directed in the instructions that follow.

Use flesh to paint handle and domed furniture plug.

Use gold to paint star. When dry, outline star with marker.

**HAIR/BEARD:** Cut a 4-inch length of doll hair or yarn and hold it between your middle and ring fingers. Wrap additional yarn around all four fingers eight times. Cut yarn. Tie off in center with the 4-inch piece. Cut through loops at opposite sides. Glue center of bundle to top of handle for hair.

Create a bundle for beard the same as for hair, except wrap yarn around your fingers 20 times instead of eight.

**HAT:** Trace enlarged hat pattern onto tracing paper with pencil. Cut out following outline of hat pattern.

Fold plaid fabric in half lengthwise with right sides together. Pin hat pattern to fabric with grain lines matching. Sew around hat, leaving opening where shown on pattern. Remove pattern. Trim excess fabric, leaving a narrow seam outside stitching. Turn hat inside out.

Insert one end of wire through the hole in top of handle and twist the end back around the wire to hold, leaving

# Santa Keeps Eyes Peeled for Napkins

*YOU SAY POTATO, but Irene Wegener of Corning, New York says craft project! She turned an old potato masher into a jolly napkin holder—and conversation piece—for the holidays.*

**MATERIALS NEEDED:**
Pattern on this page
Tracing paper and pencil
Wire potato masher with wooden handle
3-inch x 15-inch piece of red-and-green plaid fabric
All-purpose thread to match fabric
1-inch x 4-inch piece of cotton quilt batting
1/2-inch-high wooden star
3-inch length of artificial green
    holly garland
12-inch length of 19-gauge
    craft wire
1/4-inch domed furniture plug
Drill with 1/4-inch bit
Sandpaper
Water container

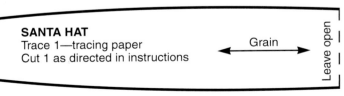

**SANTA HAT**
Trace 1—tracing paper
Cut 1 as directed in instructions

Grain

Leave open

Use photocopier to enlarge pattern 200%

about 10 inches of wire extending from top of handle.

Slip hat over end of wire and glue bottom edge of hat to top of handle.

Wrap piece of quilt batting around bottom of hat, positioning the ends in back. Glue as needed to hold.

Glue gold star to tip of hat.

Glue circle of holly garland to cuff of hat. Let dry.

Shape end of hat as shown in photo at far left.

FINISHING: Dip end of paintbrush handle into black.

Hold hair away from face and add two small dots for eyes.

Dip brush into blush and wipe excess paint onto paper towel. Hold hair away from face. With a nearly dry brush and a circular motion, add cheeks and color to nose.

Dip toothpick into white and add a tiny dot to each eye.

Use marker to add eyebrows.

Glue center of beard below Santa's nose. When dry, cut ends to shape beard.

Place napkins in base of potato masher. ✳

# Tabletops Sparkle With Starry Bowl

*THE SKY'S THE LIMIT when you use clay to embellish a plain bowl. Designed by Sandy Rollinger of Apollo, Pennsylvania, this decorative container is perfect for filling with ornaments.*

MATERIALS NEEDED:
Patterns on this page
Tracing paper and pencil
Smooth clear glass bowl (Sandy used a 10-inch-diamenter bowl)
Glass cleaner and soft cloth
White oven-bake clay (Sandy used Whipped Cream Studio Sculpey Clay)
Clay roller
Plastic mat
Powdered pigment (Sandy used Jacquard Pearl-Ex Pearl White 651)
Swirl pattern rubber stamp or texture sheet
Clay oven and foil-lined baking tray
Craft knife
Frosted glass finish
Newspaper
Clear flat-back beads (Sandy used Darice Luster Gems)
Toothpick
Ruler

FINISHED SIZE: Bowl shown has a 10-inch diameter.

DIRECTIONS:
Clean outside of bowl with glass cleaner and cloth. Place bowl upside down on foil-lined baking tray.

Trace star patterns separately onto tracing paper with pencil. Cut out patterns.

Condition clay. Roll clay out to a 1/4-inch thickness.

Apply powdered pigment over rolled clay. Press stamp or texture sheet onto clay to make impressions and remove.

Place star patterns on clay and use craft knife to cut out five large stars and five small stars.

Use your fingers to gently curve tips of each star.

Press each star onto outside of bowl where desired.

Bake bowl and clay stars at 275 degrees for 10 minutes following clay manufacturer's instructions. Let cool.

Pop each star off of bowl and set stars aside.

Clean outside of bowl with glass cleaner and soft cloth.

Place bowl upside down on newspaper-covered surface.

Following spray manufacturer's instructions, spray entire outside of bowl with frosted glass finish. Let dry. Repeat until desired look is achieved.

Apply a small amount of glue to the back of each star and glue stars to outside of bowl where desired. Let dry.

Referring to photo below for position, apply a thin bead of glue to outside of bowl. Roll a tiny amount of unbaked clay on the tip of toothpick and use to pick up a flat-back bead. Place bead over glue.

Add beads around entire bowl in the same way, creating swirl designs next to stars. Let dry. ✳

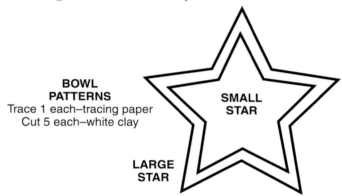

BOWL PATTERNS
Trace 1 each–tracing paper
Cut 5 each–white clay

SMALL STAR

LARGE STAR

## Nativity Puppets Are Child's Play

*SET THE STAGE for fun by letting youngsters act out their own Christmas story. In Apollo, Pennsylvania, Sandy Rollinger used plastic spoons to create Mary, Joseph and Baby Jesus.*

**MATERIALS NEEDED** (for all):
Three white plastic spoons
Felt—9-inch x 12-inch piece or scraps each of blue, light grey, dark grey, pink, turquoise and white
Two 6-inch lengths of black chenille stem
Gold metallic chenille stem—one 3-inch length and two 4-inch lengths
12-inch length of brown wire-free chenille or 15mm chenille stem
Six 1/4-inch glue-on wiggle eyes
Three 1/8-inch pink pom-poms
Fine-line permanent markers—red and black
Ruler
Craft glue
Powdered cosmetic blush and cotton swab
Scissors

**FINISHED SIZE:** Joseph and Mary puppets measure about 6 inches high x 3-1/2 inches wide. Baby Jesus puppet measures about 6 inches high x 2 inches wide.

**DIRECTIONS:**
Cut three 3-1/2-inch squares of pink felt. Glue each piece to the back side of a spoon, wrapping the edges around and gluing them to the bowl of spoon. Trim excess. Let dry.

**BABY JESUS:** Cut a 1-inch x 12-inch strip of white felt. Wrap strip around a spoon, leaving about 3/4 inch of the pink felt showing at the top. Glue in place. Let dry.

Cut a 3-inch length of brown wire-free chenille or chenille stem and glue around top of spoon for hair. Let dry.

Form a 3-inch length of gold chenille stem into a circle for halo. Glue halo to back of head. Let dry.

Using cotton swab, apply blush in a circular motion to add cheeks to face.

Glue wiggle eyes and a pom-pom nose to face. Let dry.

Use red marker to add mouth.

**JOSEPH:** Cut a 3-1/2-inch x 4-inch piece of dark grey felt for robe. Overlap the short edges about 1/4 inch and glue together to hold. Slip robe over handle of spoon with seam in back. Wrap a 6-inch length of black chenille stem around the robe and handle about 1 inch from the top edge of robe. Twist ends of chenille stem together in front to hold and coil the ends. Apply a bit of glue to handle to hold robe in place. Let dry.

Cut a 3-inch x 4-inch piece of light grey felt for head covering. Center and glue one short edge along top front of Joseph's head, folding remainder of piece over top of head to the back. Fold the top corners down and glue along sides of head. Let dry.

Cut a 3-inch length of brown wire-free chenille or chenille stem and glue to bottom edge of face for beard. Let dry.

Form a 4-inch length of gold chenille stem into a circle for halo. Glue halo to top of head. Let dry.

Using cotton swab, apply blush in a circular motion to add cheeks to face.

Glue wiggle eyes and a pom-pom nose to face. Let dry.

Use red marker to add mouth.

**MARY:** Cut a 3-1/2-inch x 4-inch piece of blue felt for robe. Overlap the short edges about 1/4 inch and glue together to hold. Slip robe over handle of spoon with seam in back. Wrap a 6-inch length of black chenille stem around the robe and handle about 1 inch from the top edge of robe. Twist ends of chenille stem together in front to hold and coil the ends. Apply a bit of glue to handle to hold robe in place. Let dry.

Cut a 3-inch square of turquoise felt for head covering. Use scissors to round off all corners. Center and glue one edge along top front of Mary's head, folding remainder of piece over top of head to the back. Fold the top corners down and glue to top of head. Let dry.

Cut a 6-inch length of brown wire-free chenille or chenille stem and glue around face for hair. Let dry.

Form a 4-inch length of gold chenille stem into a circle for halo. Glue halo to top of head. Let dry.

Using cotton swab, apply blush in a circular motion to add cheeks to face.

Glue wiggle eyes and a pom-pom nose to face. Let dry.

Use red marker to add mouth.

Use black marker to add eyebrows. ✷

# Kick Back with Fun Striped Socks

*YOU'LL STEP UP to holiday gift-giving with this cozy knit footwear from Debbie Slaback of Longview, Texas. Everyone will love the bright colors and casual striped pattern.*

## MATERIALS NEEDED:
One ball of sock yarn
Set of four size 1 (2.25mm) double-pointed needles
Measuring tape or ruler
Yarn or tapestry needle
Scissors

**GAUGE:** 17 stitches and 23 rows = 2 inches. To save time, take time to check gauge.

**FINISHED SIZE:** Directions are for Women's size Small socks with changes for Women's Medium and Large sizes in parentheses.

## DIRECTIONS:
**TOE:** Cast on 12 sts on one needle.

Using new needle, k across sts, knitting into the front and back of every st: 24 sts.

Pinch the cast-on edge between your thumb and index finger and gently slide the needle out of the sts. The sts will spring to the front and back alternately. While holding the cast-on edge, slip one needle into the sts in the front and another needle into the sts in the back. You will have 12 sts on each needle.

**Round 1:** K 1, k 1 into front and back of next st, k across to last two sts, k 1 into front and back of next st, k 1. Work the same across both needles.

**Round 2:** K around.

Place sts evenly on three needles.

Repeat Rounds 1 and 2 until you have 28 (32 for medium, 36 for large) sts on each needle. This completes the toe of the sock. Mark 26 (30, 34) sts for the top of the sock and the remaining 30 (34, 38) sts for the sole.

K around for 6 (7, 8) inches from toe.

**GUSSET: Round 1:** K across 26 (30, 34) sts (top of sock), k 1, k 1 into front and back of first sole st, k across to last two sts, k 1 into front and back of next st, k 1.

**Round 2:** K around.

Repeat Rounds 1 and 2 until you have 56 (64, 72) sts.

**TURNING HEEL:** Work sts on sole sts only. The sts for the top of the sock will not be worked while turning the heel of sock.

---

**Row 1:** K 29 (33, 35), ssk, k 1, turn.
**Row 2:** Sl 1, p 3 (5, 7), p2tog, p 1, turn.
**Row 3:** Sl 1, k 4 (6, 8), ssk, k 1, turn.
**Row 4:** Sl 1, p 5 (7, 9), p2tog, p 1, turn.
**Row 5:** Sl 1, k 6 (8, 10), ssk, k 1, turn.

Continue in this manner until all the sts have been worked and you have 30 (34, 36) sts on needle.

Work in the round on all sts (both needles) for 10 rows.

**CUFF: Rounds 1-4:** K 2, p 2 around.

**Round 5:** ° K2tog leaving st on needle, k 1 in st closest to the tip of the needle, then pull both sts off needle, p 2; repeat from ° around.

Repeat Rounds 1-5 until cuff measures 3 inches.

**SEWN BIND OFF:** Cut a piece of yarn that is three times the distance around the cuff. Thread yarn onto the yarn or tapestry needle. Working from right to left, ° insert yarn or tapestry needle purl-wise through the first two sts on the knitting needle and draw the yarn through. Bring yarn or tapestry needle knit-wise through first st, pull the yarn through and sl this st off the knitting needle. Repeat from ° around the top of the cuff. Fasten off. ❋

---

| ABBREVIATIONS | | | |
|---|---|---|---|
| k | knit | st(s) | stitch(es) |
| p | purl | ssk | slip, slip, knit |
| sl | slip | tog | together |
| * Instructions following asterisk are repeated as directed. | | | |

## Branch Out with Tree Wall Quilt

*THIS PINE DESIGN lets you enjoy a Christmas tree on your wall, too! Notes Petaluma, California crafter Loretta Mateik, "You could add other appliques as well, such as ornaments."*

**MATERIALS NEEDED:**
Patterns on next page
Paper-backed fusible web
Tracing paper (optional)
Pencil
44-inch-wide 100% cotton fabrics—1/4 yard of gold on green print for inner border, 1/4 yard each of two different red prints for outer border, 1/4 yard each of three different green prints for outer border, 1/2 yard of different green print for tree applique, 2/3 yard of Christmas word print for background, 1-1/8 yards of fabric for backing, 1/3 yard of green solid for binding, 1/8 yard of gold solid for star and lights, 1/8 yard of dark green solid for tree trunk and 1/8 yard each of green solid, dark red solid and red solid for lights
36-inch square of lightweight quilt batting
All-purpose thread to match fabrics
Six-strand embroidery floss—dark green, green, gold, light green and red to match red solid fabrics
Embroidery needle
Quilter's marking pen or pencil
Quilter's ruler
Rotary cutter and mat
Standard sewing supplies

**FINISHED SIZE:** Wall hanging measures about 35-1/2 inches square.

**DIRECTIONS:**
**CUTTING:** From word print, cut one 20-1/2-inch square for background.

From green print for inner border, cut two 3-inch x 20-1/2-inch strips and two 3-inch x 25-1/2-inch strips.

From each of the two red prints for outer border, cut six 5-1/2-inch squares.

From each of the three green prints for outer border, cut four 5-1/2-inch squares.

From green solid for binding, cut four 2-1/2-inch-wide crosswise strips.

From backing fabric, cut one 40-inch square and one 3-inch x 33-inch strip for hanging sleeve.

**PIECING:** Do all piecing with right sides of fabric together, matching thread and an accurate 1/4-inch seam. Press seams toward darker fabric.

Sew a 3-inch x 20-1/2-inch inner border strip to opposite sides of the 20-1/2-inch-square Christmas word fabric for background. Open and press seams toward inner border.

Sew a 3-inch x 25-1/2-inch inner border strip to top and bottom edges of the Christmas word fabric for background.

Referring to photo at left above, lay out the 5-1/2-inch green and red print squares right side up for outer border.

Omitting the corner squares, sew the top row of squares together as planned. Repeat with bottom row of squares, making two pieced strips.

Sew a pieced strip to top and bottom edges of inner border.

Sew the remaining side squares together, making two pieced strips.

Sew a pieced strip to opposite sides of inner border, carefully matching corners.

**APPLIQUES:** Trace all light patterns and the enlarged star, tree and trunk patterns separately onto paper side of fusible web, leaving at least a 1/2-inch space between patterns. Cut patterns apart, leaving a margin of paper around each.

Following manufacturer's instructions, fuse patterns onto wrong side of fabrics as directed on patterns. Let cool.

Cut out shapes following outline of patterns. Remove paper backing.

Referring to photo for position, place tree and trunk on front of background of wall hanging, overlapping the trunk as shown on pattern. Fuse tree and trunk in place.

Fuse star to top of tree.

Fuse tree lights to tree, then fuse a gold base to each, overlapping the lights as shown on pattern.

Fuse border lights to outer border and fuse a gold base to each light the same as before.

*(Continued on page 104)*

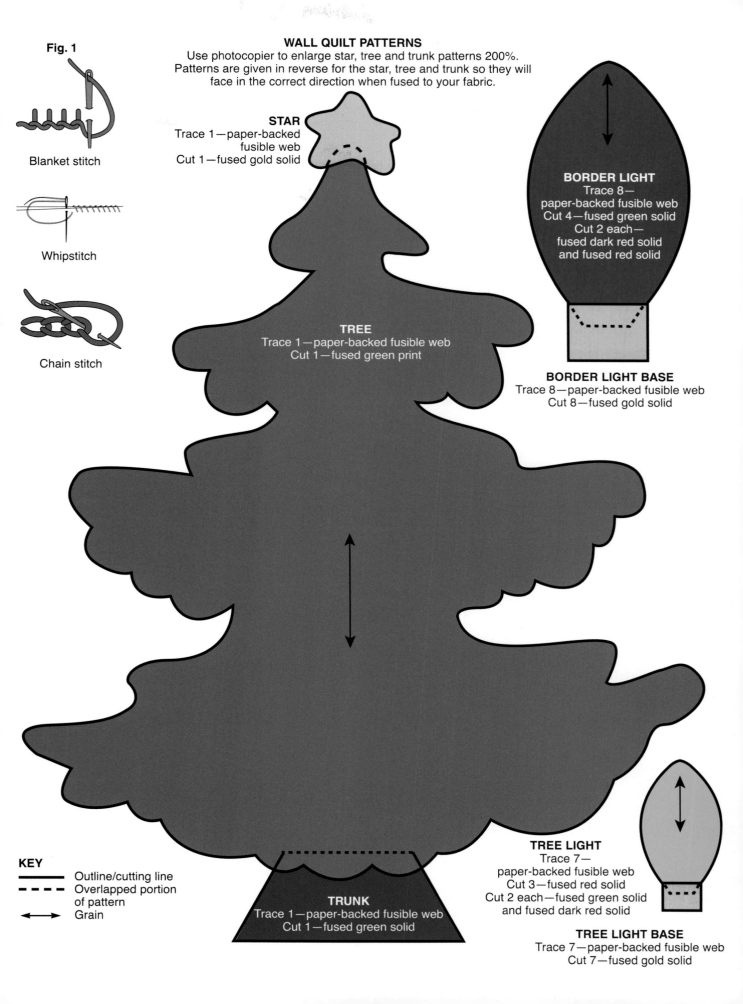

**Fig. 1**

Blanket stitch

Whipstitch

Chain stitch

**WALL QUILT PATTERNS**
Use photocopier to enlarge star, tree and trunk patterns 200%.
Patterns are given in reverse for the star, tree and trunk so they will
face in the correct direction when fused to your fabric.

**STAR**
Trace 1—paper-backed
fusible web
Cut 1—fused gold solid

**TREE**
Trace 1—paper-backed fusible web
Cut 1—fused green print

**BORDER LIGHT**
Trace 8—
paper-backed fusible web
Cut 4—fused green solid
Cut 2 each—
fused dark red solid
and fused red solid

**BORDER LIGHT BASE**
Trace 8—paper-backed fusible web
Cut 8—fused gold solid

**TREE LIGHT**
Trace 7—
paper-backed fusible web
Cut 3—fused red solid
Cut 2 each—fused green solid
and fused dark red solid

**TREE LIGHT BASE**
Trace 7—paper-backed fusible web
Cut 7—fused gold solid

**TRUNK**
Trace 1—paper-backed fusible web
Cut 1—fused green solid

**KEY**
⎯⎯⎯ Outline/cutting line
- - - - Overlapped portion
of pattern
↔ Grain

**EMBROIDERY:** Separate six-strand floss and use the number of strands indicated in the instructions that follow. Refer to Fig. 1 on page 103 for stitch illustrations.

Using two strands of matching green floss, blanket-stitch around tree and trunk.

Using two strands of gold floss, blanket-stitch around star.

Using one strand of matching floss, blanket-stitch around each of the lightbulbs.

Using one strand of gold floss, whipstitch around the gold base of each bulb.

Using quilter's marking pen or pencil, draw lines between the lights on the tree so design resembles a string of lights. Repeat on outer border. Use two strands of dark green floss to chain-stitch over lines.

**QUILTING:** Place backing fabric wrong side up on a flat surface. Center batting on top of backing.

Center pieced top right side up on batting and smooth out all wrinkles. Baste layers together.

Hand- or machine-quilt as desired.

Machine stitch 1/8 inch from outer edges of pieced top. Remove basting.

**BINDING:** Sew short ends of binding strips together diagonally to make one long strip. Trim and press seams open.

Press one short end diagonally 1/4 inch to wrong side.

Press strip in half lengthwise with wrong sides together.

Sew binding strip to right side of pieced top with edges matching and a 1/4-inch seam, mitering corners.

Fold binding to back, encasing raw edges.

Hand-sew fold of binding to back of quilt, covering seam.

**HANGING SLEEVE:** Hem the short edges of the 3-inch x 33-inch hanging sleeve piece.

Fold hanging sleeve in half lengthwise with wrong sides together. Sew long edges together with a narrow seam to make a tube. Press tube flat and seam open.

Pin hanging sleeve centered along top back of wall hanging. Hand-sew folds of hanging sleeve to backing. ✳

# *Cozy Up to a Snowman Pillow*

*THE COMFORTS of a holiday home can start with this charming accent pillow from Loretta Mateik of Petaluma, California. She used needle felting and embroidery to create the design.*

**MATERIALS NEEDED:**
Patterns on next page
Tracing paper and pencil
1/2 yard of 60-inch-wide dark green
    sweatshirt fabric
Matching all-purpose thread
1-1/2 yards of upholstery cording
Wool roving—small amount each of black,
    lime green, orange, red and white
Felting needle and mat
Six-strand embroidery floss—dark brown,
    orange and white
Embroidery needle
Light transfer paper
Two 3/8-inch black sew-through buttons
12-inch square pillow form
Standard sewing supplies

**FINISHED SIZE:** Pillow measures about 12 inches square. Needle-felted design measures about 9-1/2 inches high x 4-1/4 inches wide.

**DIRECTIONS:**
From sweatshirt fabric, cut two 13-inch squares for front and back of pillow. Also cut four 2-inch x 18-inch lengthwise strips for piping.

Trace snowman and snowflake patterns onto tracing paper with pencil. Place snowman pattern on one square of sweatshirt fabric for pillow front. Slip transfer paper between pattern and fabric. Trace over lines with pencil to transfer design.

Referring to the photo at bottom far left for position, transfer three snowflakes the same as before.

**NEEDLE FELTING:** Place white wool roving inside the snowman outline for the white areas, twisting strands slightly so edges are somewhat smooth and follow the outline of the shape.

Place pillow front on felting mat. Insert and remove felting needle with an up-and-down motion to lock the fibers together. Add more roving and continue needle felting as needed to fill in the snowman shape.

In the same way, add the orange nose, black hat, black eye and red-and-green scarf.

**EMBROIDERY:** Separate brown six-strand floss and thread embroidery needle with three strands. Chain-stitch each stick arm. See Fig. 1 at top far right for stitch illustration.

In the same way, use white floss to add the three snowflakes and snow line below snowman. Use orange floss to add curl to tip of nose.

Use black floss to sew buttons to snowman.

**PILLOW: Piping:** Sew short ends of piping strips together with a diagonal seam. Trim each to a 1/4-inch seam allowance. Press seams open.

Place cording on center of wrong side of piping strip. Wrap fabric around strip and use a zipper foot to sew along length of strip close to cording, encasing cording.

Starting at the bottom of the pillow, pin piping strip to pillow front with edges matching. Sew around pillow, stitching just inside previous stitching on piping strip and clipping piping strip at each corner. Trim ends of cording so they meet at the center bottom. Fold back piping strip and lap it over the beginning of the strip. Sew ends in place.

**Finishing:** Pin pillow front and back pieces together with right sides together and edges matching.

Sew around pillow with a 1/2-inch seam, leaving an opening for turning. Trim corners diagonally and turn pillow right side out.

Insert pillow form. Turn the raw edges of the opening in and hand-sew opening closed. ✳

**PILLOW PATTERNS**
Trace 1 each—
tracing paper

**Fig. 1**

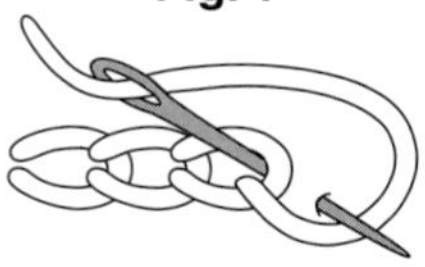

Chain stitch

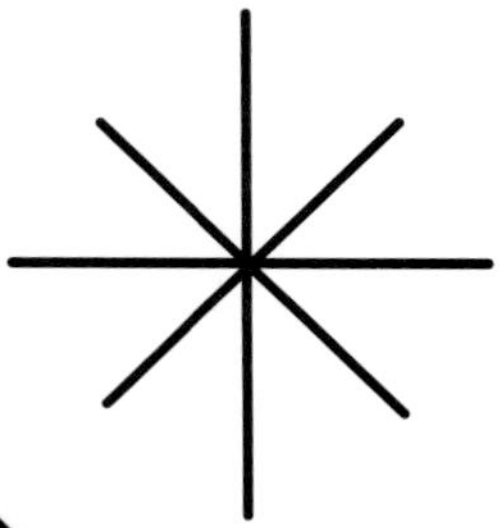

**SNOWFLAKE**
Stitch as directed
in instructions

**SNOWMAN**
Needle-felt and stitch as
directed in instructions

# Welcome Christmas With Holiday Homes

YOU'LL BUILD fun when you make these whimsical houses from Mary Ayres of Boyce, Virginia. Use them as ornaments—or as charming gift boxes for gift cards or small items.

**MATERIALS NEEDED** (for all):
Cardboard matchboxes—one large (4-3/4 inches high x 2-1/2 inches wide x 1-1/2 inches deep) and two small (2-1/8 inches high x 1-1/2 inches wide x 1/2 inch deep)
5-inch square of 1/4-inch-thick foam core
Patterned paper (Mary used Phoebe by Basic Grey)—assorted pink, blue and green prints
Card stock—white and black
Nine pewter mini brads
3/8-inch silver jingle bell
6-inch length of 1/8-inch-wide fuchsia satin ribbon
Krylon Metallic Spray Paint—Silver Metallic
Paper glue (Mary used Beacon Adhesives Zip Dry)
Black fine-line marker or computer with printer
Small piece of household sponge
Scissors
Ruler
Ink pads—bright pink, blue and green
1/16-inch round hole punch
Fishing line for hanging loops (optional)
Small flat paintbrush
Ultra-fine iridescent glitter

**FINISHED SIZE:** Each small house measures about 4 inches high x 3-1/4 inches wide. Large house measures about 7-1/4 inches high x 4-1/2 inches wide.

**DIRECTIONS:**
Refer to the photo above as a guide while assembling as directed in the instructions that follow.

Use sponge piece and matching ink color to antique edges of all print paper pieces after cutting out shapes as directed in the instructions that follow.

**SMALL "NOEL" HOUSE:** Slide inside box from matchbox cover.

Spray entire box with spray paint following manufacturer's instructions. Let dry.

If desired, use paper punch to make two holes in the corners on one short side of silver box for a hanging loop.

Cut a 2-1/8-inch x 4-1/2-inch piece of green print paper to fit around matchbox cover.

Cut a 1/2-inch x 1-inch piece of pink print paper for door. Glue door to center of bottom edge of cover.

Cut a 1/2-inch x 2-inch piece of blue print paper and a 1/2-inch square of white paper. Glue the white square to the center of the blue rectangle for window and shutters.

Use black marker to draw panes on window. Crease shutters at edge of window. Glue window above door.

Use punch to make a hole in door and attach a brad in hole for doorknob.

Glue green paper cover around matchbox cover with the edges matching and the door and window centered on front of matchbox cover.

Cut a 1-3/4-inch square of foam core and cut in half diagonally for triangle under roof. Save one triangle for small "Love" house.

Cut a same-size triangle of pink print paper. With edges matching, glue pink triangle to foam core triangle.

Make another window with shutters the same as before.

Glue window and shutters to center of triangle.

Insert silver part of box inside cover.

Glue foam triangle to top 3/8 inch of silver box.

Cut two 1/4-inch x 3-inch strips of white card stock. Glue strips to top of foam triangle for roof, leaving ends of strips extending beyond bottom edges of roof. Roll ends of strips.

Dab glue on top of roof strips and along bottom edges of windowpanes. While still wet, sprinkle glitter on glue.

Using marker or computer, print "Noel" on white card stock and cut out, leaving a 1/4-inch margin of paper around word. Apply pink ink to edges. Attach strip inside box with brads so that the word is visible when box is opened about 1 inch.

If desired, cut a 10-inch piece of fishing line, insert through holes in top of box and knot ends for hanging loop.

**SMALL "LOVE" HOUSE:** Follow the instructions for making the "Noel" house, making the following changes:

Use light blue print paper for wrapping matchbox cover, bright blue print paper for door, pink print paper for shutters and green print paper for triangle under roof. Print

"Love" on white card stock.

**LARGE HOUSE:** Follow the instructions for making the "Noel" house, making the following changes:

Use a 4-3/4-inch x 9-inch rectangle of light pink print paper for wrapping matchbox cover, a 1-inch x 2-1/2-inch piece of green print paper for door, two 3/4-inch x 1-1/2-inch rectangles of blue print paper for shutters and two 3/4-inch squares of white paper for windows. Cut a 2-1/2-inch square of foam core, cut in half diagonally and cover one triangle with a same-size piece of bright pink print paper for triangle under roof. Use two 1/4-inch x 5-inch strips of white card stock for roof. Print "Happy Holidays" on white card stock.

**Finishing:** Cut a 1-inch square of foam core, cut in half diagonally and cover one triangle with a same-size piece of black card stock for triangle above door. Glue above door.

Cut two 1/4-inch x 2-1/2 inch strips of white paper and attach to triangle above door the same as for roof.

Thread fuchsia ribbon through jingle bell and tie ends in a bow. Glue bow to triangle above door. ✳

---

# Poinsettias Perk Up Plain Glass Vase

*CREATE YOUR OWN seasonal candle holder with this simple design from Jenny Hensgen of Waterford, Wisconsin. Her glittery blooms turn ho-hum glassware into a holiday stunner.*

## MATERIALS NEEDED:
Pattern on this page
Tracing paper and pencil
8-1/2 x 11-inch piece of white paper
10-inch-tall x 6-inch-diameter clear glass vase
Tape
Clear-drying craft glue (Jenny used Aileen's Tacky Glue)
Toothpicks
Fine glass glitter (Jenny used Martha Stewart Glitter)—clear, gold and green
Soft bristle paintbrush

**FINISHED SIZE:** Vase shown is 10 inches high x 6 inches in diameter. Pattern may be enlarged or reduced to fit vases of different sizes.

**EDITOR'S NOTE:** To clean, wipe decorated vase with a damp cloth. Do not submerse vase in water.

## DIRECTIONS:
Trace enlarged pattern onto tracing paper with pencil.

Tape pattern to inside of glass vase.

Using toothpick, apply glue to vase over a small gold section of pattern. While still wet, sprinkle gold glitter over glue. Shake off excess glitter. Let dry until no longer tacky.

Repeat to add the remaining gold areas of design to vase. Move pattern around vase as needed.

In the same way, apply white glitter to vase where shown on pattern.

In the same way, apply green glitter to vase where shown on pattern.

Brush outside of vase with soft bristle brush to remove excess glitter. Let vase dry at least 24 hours before using. ✳

**POINSETTIA PATTERN**
Trace 1—tracing paper

Use photocopier to enlarge pattern 200%

# *Cute Clay Trims Break the Mold*

*TO ROLL OUT some delightfully different ornaments, try the cute Santa and colorful tree from Sandy Rollinger of Apollo, Pennsylvania. They're sure to brighten up branches.*

**MATERIALS NEEDED** (for both):
Patterns on this page
Tracing paper and pencil
Oven-bake clay (Sandy used Studio by Sculpey clay)—
    Blush, Denim, Fuchsia Fury, Lemon Drop, Peapod, Poppy and Whipped Cream
Plastic mat
Clay blade or craft knife
Clay roller
Clay oven and foil-lined baking tray
Toothpick
Two 10-inch lengths of 1/8-inch-wide red satin ribbon
Two 1/8-inch glue-on wiggle eyes
Ruler
Craft glue
Scissors

**FINISHED SIZE:** Excluding hanging loop, Santa ornament measures about 3-1/4 inches high x 2 inches wide and tree ornament measures about 3 inches high x 1-3/4 inches wide.

**DIRECTIONS:**
Refer to the photo at left as a guide while assembling the ornaments as directed in the instructions that follow.

Condition clay. Use clay roller to roll out clay to an 1/8-inch thickness on plastic mat.

**SANTA ORNAMENT:** Trace Santa hat, face and beard patterns onto tracing paper with pencil. Cut clay shapes as directed on patterns.

From Whipped Cream clay, cut a 3/8-inch x 1-1/8-inch rectangle for hat trim and two 1/8-inch x 3/8-inch rectangles for eyebrows. Also cut a 1-inch x 3/8-inch rectangle, then cut it in half diagonally for the two mustache pieces.

Use toothpick to make wiggly vertical lines on the beard.

Place hat, face and beard pieces on foil-lined tray, making sure edges of pieces are touching where shown on patterns.

Press hat trim over the seam between hat and face.

Roll a pea-size ball of Whipped Cream. Press ball to top of hat and flatten it a bit for pom-pom.

Use end of toothpick to make tiny indentations in hat trim and pom-pom.

Press eyebrows to face below hat trim.

Roll three pea-size balls of Fuchsia Fury. Flatten two of the balls and press them onto face for cheeks.

Press mustache pieces over seam between face and beard.

Press the remaining ball of Fuchsia Fury between the mus-

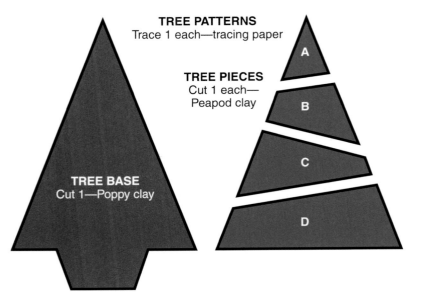

tache pieces for the nose.

Bake assembled Santa ornament following clay manufacturer's instructions. Let cool.

Glue wiggle eyes to Santa's face.

**TREE ORNAMENT:** Trace tree base and four tree piece (A, B, C and D) patterns onto tracing paper with pencil. Cut clay shapes as directed on patterns.

Place tree base on foil-lined tray. Place the four tree pieces on top of the tree base with outside edges matching, leaving a space between each piece so the base shows through.

Roll five 1/8-inch balls of Lemon Drop, five 1/8-inch balls of Fuchsia Fury and nine 1/8-inch balls of Denim clay for ornaments. Press ornaments onto green areas of tree and flatten each a bit.

Bake assembled tree ornament following clay manufacturer's instructions. Let cool.

**FINISHING:** Glue ends of a ribbon piece together on top back of each ornament for hanging loop. Let dry. ✳

# Scrappy Gift Boxes Are Extra Special

*IF YOUR FABRIC STASH is overflowing, turn your scraps into stuffed packages that can accent any spot. "They're fun and easy to sew," says Loretta Mateik of Petaluma, California.*

**MATERIALS NEEDED** (for all):
Scraps each of black print and cream print (or 1/6 yard of 44-inch-wide fabric each)
Scraps of red print (or 1/4 yard of 44-inch-wide fabric)
All-purpose thread to match fabrics
Rotary cutter and mat
Quilter's ruler
Ribbons in coordinating colors
Polyester stuffing
Standard sewing supplies

**FINISHED SIZE:** Excluding ribbons, red gift box measures about 10-1/2 inches high x 6 inches across, black gift box measures about 4-1/2 inches square and cream gift box measures about 3-1/2 inches high x 2-1/2 inches across.

**DIRECTIONS:**
From red print, cut four 6-1/2-inch x 11-inch rectangles and two 6-1/2-inch squares.

From black print, cut six 5-inch squares.

From cream print, cut four 3-inch x 4-inch rectangles and two 4-inch squares.

Do all stitching with right sides facing, edges matching, 1/4-inch seam and matching thread.

**RED GIFT BOX:** Sew the four 6-1/2-inch x 11-inch rectangles together along the 11-inch edges with three seams. Press the seams open. Press 1/4 inch along the remaining long edges to wrong side.

Pin one side of a 6-1/2-inch square to one side of joined sides. Start sewing 1/4 inch in from edge. Sew across to next seam. Leave needle down and pivot top piece to align with the bottom piece. Sew to next seam as before. Continue in this way to attach square.

Repeat on other end.

Turn right side out and stuff gift box. With matching thread, hand-sew edges of remaining seam closed.

**BLACK GIFT BOX:** Sew the four 5-inch squares together with three seams. Press the seams open. Press 1/4 inch along the remaining side edges to wrong side.

Pin one side of a 5-inch square to one side of joined sides. Start sewing 1/4 inch in from edge. Sew across to next seam. Leave needle down and pivot top piece to align with the bottom piece. Sew to next seam as before. Continue in this way to attach square.

Repeat on other end.

Turn right side out and stuff gift box. With matching thread, hand-sew edges of remaining seam closed.

**CREAM GIFT BOX:** Sew the four 3-inch x 4-inch rectangles together along the 3-inch edges with three seams. Press the seams open. Press 1/4 inch along the remaining short edges to wrong side.

Pin one side of a 4-inch square to one side of joined sides. Start sewing 1/4 inch in from edge. Sew across to next seam. Leave needle down and pivot top piece to align with the bottom piece. Sew to next seam as before. Continue in this way to attach square.

Repeat on other end.

Turn right side out and stuff gift box. With matching thread, hand-sew edges of remaining seam closed.

**FINISHING:** Wrap coordinating ribbon around each gift package as desired and tie ends in a bow. ✳

## *Pieced Runner Has Christmas Sewn Up*

YOU'LL UNCOVER *a seasonal standout when you stitch this quilted table topper from CW Craft Editor Jane Craig. "It's an easy project that's suitable for beginners," she notes.*

**MATERIALS NEEDED:**
44-inch-wide 100% cotton fabrics—1/4 yard of green print and 1/4 yard each of off-white print and red-and-green print
20-inch x 35-inch piece of coordinating fabric for backing
All-purpose thread to match fabrics
20-inch x 35-inch piece of lightweight quilt batting
Rotary cutter and mat
Quilter's ruler
Standard sewing supplies

**FINISHED SIZE:** Runner measures about 31 inches long x 16 inches wide.

**DIRECTIONS:**
Pre-wash fabrics, washing each color separately. If rinse water is discolored, wash again until rinse water runs clear. Dry and press fabrics.

CUTTING: Use rotary cutter and quilter's ruler to cut fabrics as directed in the instructions that follow.

From off-white print, cut thirty-six 2-inch squares and thirteen 2-inch x 5-inch rectangles.

From red-and-green print, cut forty-four 2-inch squares.

From green print, cut two 3-inch x 11-inch strips and two 3-inch x 31-1/2-inch strips for borders. Also cut three-2-inch x 44-inch strips for binding.

PIECING: Do all stitching with right sides of fabrics together, edges even, matching thread and an accurate 1/4-inch seam. Press seams toward darker fabrics.

End block (make 2): Referring to Fig. 1 below left, lay out off-white and red-and-green squares right side up in a checkerboard pattern. Sew squares in each row together and then sew rows together, carefully matching corners.

Sew a red-and-green square to each short end of four off-white rectangles. Sew a pieced strip to two sides of pieced checkerboard.

Sew an off-white square to opposite ends of remaining pieced strips. Sew a pieced strip to top and bottom of pieced checkerboard to complete the end block.

Repeat to make second end block.

Center block (make 1): Sew long edges of five off-white rectangles together to make a 5-inch x 8-inch pieced rectangle for center block.

Sew a red-and-green square to opposite sides of each remaining off-white square.

Sew the pieced strips to the opposite short edges of the pieced rectangle.

Finishing: Sew an end block to each long edge of the center block.

QUILTING: Place backing fabric wrong side up on a flat surface. Center batting on top of backing.

Center pieced runner right side up on batting and smooth out all wrinkles. Baste layers together.

Hand- or machine-quilt as desired.

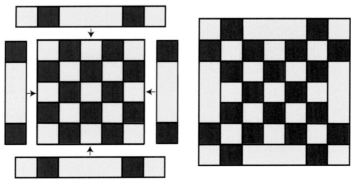

**Fig. 1**
Piecing each end block

**Fig. 2**
Piecing center block

Machine stitch 1/8 inch from outer edges of pieced top. Remove basting.

BINDING: Sew short ends of the green print binding strips together diagonally to make one long strip. Trim and press seams open.

Press one short end diagonally 1/4 inch to wrong side.

Press strip in half lengthwise with wrong sides facing.

Sew binding strip to right side of pieced top with edges matching and a 1/4-inch seam, mitering corners.

Fold binding to back, encasing raw edges.

Hand-sew the fold of binding to the back of runner, covering the seam. ✳

# Scrapbook Page Captures the Magic

*DON'T BELIEVE you have time for scrapbooking? Try this fun Christmastime design from CW Associate Editor Amy Glander. The festive layout includes plenty of space for journaling.*

## MATERIALS NEEDED:

12-inch square sheet of holiday stripe patterned paper (Amy used Karen Foster Design)

Card stock (Amy used Bazzill Basics)—two 12-inch square sheets of red solid, 5-1/2-inch x 7-1/2-inch rectangle of black solid and scrap of white solid

Round corner punch (optional)

Buttons of assorted sizes—green, red, white, pink and blue

Precut polka-dot circle about 6 inches in diameter (Amy used Making Memories)

Black stamping ink

Purchased quote on transparency to fit across bottom of page

14-inch length of 1/2-inch-wide polka-dot ribbon

2-inch circle punch

Toothpick

Craft glue or decoupage medium

Metal ring about 2 inches in diameter

Rub-on holiday message or design to fit inside ring

Scrapbook adhesive

Ruler

Scissors or paper trimmer

5-inch x 7-inch vertical photo

Black fine-line marker or computer with printer for journaling

FINISHED SIZE: Scrapbook page is 12 inches square.

## DIRECTIONS:

Refer to the photo at right as a guide while assembling as directed in the instructions that follow.

With edges matching, glue sheet of holiday stripe paper onto a sheet of red card stock. If desired, round all four corners using a corner punch.

Arrange buttons as desired across the top of scrapbook page. Glue to page using scrapbook adhesive.

Glue precut circle to the left side of page, positioning it about 3/4 inch from the left edge.

Using either black marker or computer with printer, print journaling onto red card stock, leaving enough space between lines to cut the journaling into strips.

Cut journaling into strips. Ink the edges using black stamping ink and lightly smudge the ink for a distressed look. Glue journaling strips over polka-dot circle.

Center photo on 5-1/2-inch x 7-1/2-inch black card stock piece and glue in place. Round corners of black card stock if desired. Glue assembled piece to the right side of page, slightly overlapping the polka-dot circle and right edges of journaling strips.

Cut a 2-inch x 12-inch strip of red card stock. Tear the edge along one long side of the strip. With torn edge at the bottom, glue strip about an inch below the photo and paper circle.

Cut quote to fit over the red card stock strip, leaving about 1/2 inch of transparency above the quote. Lay quote strip over the red card stock strip.

Apply adhesive to the back of the entire 14-inch length of green polka-dot ribbon. Lay the ribbon over the top 1/2 inch of the transparency and fold the ends around the edges of page, securing the ribbon and transparency to page.

Using circle punch, punch a circle from white card stock. Apply rub-on holiday message or design to circle.

Using a toothpick, apply a very thin layer of craft glue or decoupage medium to the back of the metal ring and glue ring to card stock circle.

Glue entire circle embellishment to the bottom right corner of photo. Let dry. ✳

# A Christmas I'll Never Forget...

✳ *Special Feature* ✳

## Merry Memento

I GREW UP hearing the tale of how my grandmother lost her wedding ring not long after she was married. She lived in the same house for over 50 years, and combed through it countless times hoping to find the band...never with any luck.

After Grandpa died, Grandma decided to leave their sprawling farmhouse and move to an apartment. I was walking her through the house one last time when I got the urge to take a closer look into one corner. There lay the wedding ring!

Just 3 years later, that wonderful lady passed away at holiday time. On Christmas Eve, my mother said she had a gift for me from Grandma—and dropped that priceless ring into my hands.

—Bev Olsen, Cleveland, Minnesota

## Pageant Pop-In

WHEN MY NEPHEW, Vinny, was 6 years old, he and his family attended their church Christmas pageant. While waiting for it to start, Vinny informed his father that he had to use the restroom. His father told him to hurry because the procession would be starting soon.

Minutes passed, and the family began to glance around, looking for Vinny. He didn't reappear. More minutes went by, and still Vinny didn't return. Finally, his father got up to go looking for him.

Just then, the large procession started down the aisle of the church—and there was Vinny, dressed as a bearded shepherd and carrying a staff!

It seems that, on his way to the restroom, Vinny had been mistaken for a member of the procession, quickly dressed and added to the moving throng of children. And he never said a word!

Our family will never forget Vinny's surprise reappearance that day in the Christmas pageant.

—Rosemarie Lynn, Elizabethtown, Pennsylvania

## Fa-La-La Finery

ONE YEAR, my husband and I were invited to an elegant Christmas dinner party to be held in a historic Victorian house. I decided I would make myself a special outfit just for the occasion.

While shopping at the fabric store, I discovered a beautiful Christmas-green fabric. I bought some and made a long skirt and matching vest. Trying them on, I felt quite stylish and festive.

I proudly wore the outfit to the party. But imagine my horror when I entered the dining room—only to discover that the tablecloth was made out of exactly the same fabric as my outfit!

The other party guests were kind and no one said a word, but I'm sure some of them wondered if I were meant to be the centerpiece!

I never did wear that outfit again.

—LaVerne Clabaugh, Council Bluffs, Iowa

## Home for the Holidays

AS A TEENAGER, I lived with my family on an island in the Northumberland Strait but attended school on the mainland. Transportation between the island and mainland was limited, especially during winter.

One snowy December, six other teens and I were eager to leave school and return home for Christmas break. Our only way back to the island was on a mail plane with seating for the pilot and one passenger.

There were just two of us left to transport when a blizzard bulletin was issued. My eyes filled with tears as I watched the plane being covered with a tarp. We would not be going home after all.

Somehow, word of our plight reached the island, and arrangements were made to drive us to Caribou Wharf. It was nearly dark when we saw a small boat approaching—manned by my dad and a friend of his. What a beautiful sight it was!

Our "rescuers" maneuvered the boat through the gale while we passengers huddled in the bow. Two hours and 7 miles later, we were spotted by an islander with binoculars, and the call went out that we'd made it home safely.

I'll never forget how grateful I was for that simple gift—the gift of being home for Christmas.

—Rose DeWolfe, Dartmouth, Nova Scotia

# Recipe and Craft Index